THAT
BAD
REVIEW

How to Turn 1-Star Reviews Into a 5-Star Business

Adrian Easdown

INDEPENDENT INK

First published 2018 by Independent Ink
PO Box 1638, Carindale
Queensland 4152 Australia
independentink.com.au

Cover design by Jo Hunt
Edited by Kristy Bushnell
Internal design by Independent Ink
Typeset in 11.5/15.6 pt Adobe Garamond by Post Pre-press Group, Brisbane

A catalogue record for this
book is available from the
National Library of Australia

NATIONAL
LIBRARY
OF AUSTRALIA

ISBN 978 0 9876440 1 5 (paperback)
ISBN 978 0 9876440 2 2 (epub)
ISBN 978 0 9876440 3 9 (kindle)

Disclaimer:
Any information in the book is purely the opinion of the author based on personal experience and should not be taken as business or legal advice. All material is provided for educational purposes only. We recommend to always seek the advice of a qualified professional before making any decision regarding personal and business needs.

Contents

Foreword XI

Introduction 1

    That Bad Review 3

    The Five Phases of a Bad Review 4

        Phase One: They Said What?!?

        Phase Two: I'm Crap, You're Crap, We're All Crap

        Phase Three: It's Lies, All Lies!

        Phase Four: Whose Fault is It Anyway?

        Phase Five: Round Up the Troops, It's Time to Deal

    Can You Avoid Bad Reviews?. 6

PART ONE LET'S GET STARTED

CHAPTER 1

The Big, Fat LIE About the Accommodation Industry 11

    High-risk Guests and You 12

        The Guests Who Fish for a Discount

        The Guests on a Beer Budget with Champagne Tastes

        The Guests Who Expect the Red Carpet

        The Guests Who Huff and Puff

    If You Build It, They Will Come 16

    You Can't Be Everything to Everyone 17

    A Mini Task for You. 18

CHAPTER 2

What's In It for Me?..19

    It's Not All Bad...20

    Don't Take It Too Hard.................................21

    There's No Truth to It Anyway 22

    Knowing Where Fault Lies 23

    The Benefit of Feedback...............................24

CHAPTER 3

How to Thrive and Survive Today and Every Day 26

    Social Media is Your Friend 27

    See Your Guests as People, Not Dollars 28

    Take Control of Your Reviews 29

    Build a Great Team....................................30

    Embrace Technology...................................30

    Build a Solid Backbone 31

PART TWO THE FIVE PHASES OF A BAD REVIEW

CHAPTER 4

There's Something You Should Know.........................35

    How to Tell the Good from the Bad 36

        Assigning Ratings to Your Guests

    Where Are Our Reviews Hanging Out?...................38

        TripAdvisor

        Booking.com

        Facebook

        Google Maps

        Expedia

    If I Ignore It, It Will Just Go Away 40

    A Mini Task for You....................................42

CHAPTER 5

Phase One – They Said What!?! 43

    The Seven Types of Guests Who Leave Reviews 44

        The Grateful Guest

        The Neglected Guest

        The So-so Guest

        The Firecracker Guest

        The Disorganised Guest

        The By-the-book Guest

        The 1%-er Guest

    Why Did You Say That? 48

        Sharing Is Caring

        Saying Thank You

        They Want You to Be Better

        They Want to Be Heard

        They Want to Join the Gang

    A Mini Task for You. 51

CHAPTER 6

Phase Two – I'm Crap, You're Crap, We're All Crap 52

    Feeling the Burn of Negativity 53

        Frustration and Irritation

        Take a Step Back

        Worry and Nervousness

        Remove Yourself

        Anger and Aggravation

        Embrace the Hulk

        Rejection

        Assess Yourself

        Feeling Inadequate

        You Have the Skills

A Mini Task for You. 59

Chapter 7

Phase Three – It's Lies, All Lies! 60

    Investigating Bad Reviews 61

        Make a Checklist

        Check the System

        Ask Your Team

    Dealing with Bad Reviews 63

        Never Be Defensive

        Never Be Aggressive

        Add Personality to Your Response

        Don't Get Personal

    A Resource for You. 67

Chapter 8

Phase Four – Whose Fault Is It Anyway?. 71

    Don't Brush Aside The Feedback 72

    The Many Pieces of Feedback 73

        Bad Review Item #54: 'Your toilets weren't clean.'

        Bad Review Item #102: 'Your rooms weren't clean.'

        Bad Review Item #145: 'There were too many people staying.'

        Bad Review Item #234: 'Your facilities need work.'

        Bad Review Item #336: 'Your staff are rude!'

        The Guest Was Misinformed

        The Guest Was Aggressive

    A Mini Task for You. 79

Chapter 9

Phase Five – Round Up the Troops, It's Time to Deal 81

    The R.E.V.I.E.W. Process 83

        R: Rate the Feedback

        E: Examine the Feedback

V: Visualise the Feedback

I: Implement Changes Based on Feedback

E: Evaluate the Impact of the Changes

Being Patient

Being Proactive

Continuous Evaluation

W: Winning Business

A Resource for You 89

PART THREE HOW TO AVOID BAD REVIEWS

CHAPTER 10

Social Media is Your Friend 97

Find the Best Social Media and Review Sites

for Your Business 98

Facebook

Instagram

Twitter

TripAdvisor

Booking.com

Find More Social Media Platforms 101

Decide Where to Prioritise Your Efforts 102

Include Your Team 102

Go High Tech 103

Have a Plan 103

A Mini Task for You 105

Social Media Goals

Social Media Standards

Social Media Value

Branding

Additional Considerations

CHAPTER 11

Customers Are People Too 108

   It's a Relationship, Not a Transaction 109

   How to Build Trust 110

      Just Be Yourself

      Treat Guests Like Individuals

      Be Curious About Your Guests

      Don't Be a Flake

      Ask for Feedback

      Communication Is the Key

      Recognise Feelings

      Be More than a Pretty Picture

   A Resource for You 116

      At Check-in

      During Their Stay

      At Check-out

CHAPTER 12

Grab the Bull by the Horns 118

   Find Your Promoters 119

      Step One: Guest Engagement

      Step Two: Social Media

      Step Three: Returning Guests

   The Gold-star List 121

   Roll Out the Red Carpet 121

      Create a Unique Experience

      Offer a Phenomenal Customer Experience

      Create a Loyalty Program

      Supercharge Your Loyalty Program

      Be Honest and Active

      Ask for Feedback

The Mid-stay Survey

Social Media Training

Conversations with Guests

The After-departure Survey

A Resource for You 126

Survey Caveats

Sample Questions for Your Survey

CHAPTER 13

Create Leaders, Not Followers 128

Empowering for Success. 129

Make Your Expectations Clear

Set Up One-on-ones

Have Your Team's Back

Building the Best Team 132

Be as Flexible as You Can

Always Celebrate the Wins

Invest in Your Team's Success

It's All About the Trust

A Mini Task for You. 135

CHAPTER 14

Embrace the Tech 138

Putting Your Best Digital Face Forward: Your Website 139

Make Sure Your Website is User-friendly

Make Sure Your Website is Linked to Your Booking System

Think Outside the Box. 141

Help Your Guests Embrace Tech. 141

Use Tech to Automate Your Guest Engagements 142

Email Marketing and Your Database

Use Email Automation to Create Promoters

Improve Your Customer Service with Tech

A Resource for You 145

CHAPTER 15

Can I Get a Process? 149

    What Processes Work the Best? 151

        Make Sure Everything is Documented

        Onboarding and Training Processes

        Standard Quality Processes

    Using Processes to Ensure Success 153

        Gather Feedback From Your Guests

        Listen to the Feedback

        Walk in Your Guests' Shoes

        Don't Ignore Inefficiencies

        Have a Review and Audit Procedure

    A Mini Task for You 156

PART FOUR THE LAST PART

CHAPTER 16

A Final Piece of Advice 159

Resources 163

Notes 167

From Stuart Lamont, Chief Executive Officer of the Caravan Industry Association of Australia

Humans have been providing word-of-mouth commentary on their experiences for centuries.

In today's global world we now influence and are influenced like never before, as individuals – many of whom we may never know – use online forums to share their thoughts and pass comment with a corresponding effect on the way that your potential customers, business colleagues, or even employees form an opinion towards you. In some ways as Adrian Easdown identifies, technology has provided the platform for word-of-mouth on steroids.

While we may find this confronting, information is power, and the information that comes from people's thoughts towards you should allow you to respond and to become even better. Yes, others can also see this online commentary, but how you react to feedback both positive and negative is very much factored into the decision-making process of individuals accessing online reviews.

They say sometimes that today's young leaders are fearless, and Adrian – while acknowledging his discomfort – does not back down from taking on the challenge or the unknown. Whether it be launching his own podcast, talking to industry experts, or delivering this easy-to-read book based on his own experiences, he has earned my respect for sharing knowledge so that others may learn and improve. As an industry we must encourage his brashness and those of the leaders around him in an everchanging world.

There is no doubt we can become consumed by negative feedback, particularly in small businesses, receiving criticism on something that you pour your heart and soul into, can feel like a kick in the guts. It takes a strong sense of one's self to be able to admit faults, listen to criticism and adopt change.

Through this book, help is at hand.

Adrian has done a great job taking his real-life experiences in the accommodation industry to share a refreshing outlook to how a bad review can be handled and turned into a positive.

Adrian's methodical approach to constructively interpreting negative consumer reviews in order to improve his own business practices is unveiled in this simple resource, and coupled with practical mini exercises so that you can apply the knowledge within to your own business, regardless of industry.

This humble approach to self-reflection in business is refreshing and reiterates that, at the end of the day, feedback really is a gift.

Introduction

Great Staff.!!!!!! Your office staff are the face of your company, and yours were extremely helpful, fun, and informative. Clean well run park. Great location.

~ David

There are two fundamental things you need to know about me before we get started. The first is that I jump headlong into situations that make me feel uncomfortable. For me, being comfortable means I am not pushing myself forward. It means I have become complacent in my day-to-day work and I am not growing myself or my business anymore. It means I have lost the ability to see the problems in my business that need correcting, or worse, I have chosen to ignore them.

The second thing you need to know is that I believe there is always a way to fix or address any type of situation that happens in my business. Sure, there are times when you can't see beyond the problem, but my approach is to never give up. All through this book you will see direct and indirect approaches to deal with the problems that accommodation owners and those in other service-based industries need to address. No-one said we had to tackle the problem head-on – from the side is okay too.

For 10 years now, my businesses have been dedicated to making sure that people on vacation in a hotel or caravan park have a good time. Actually, when I think about it, pretty much my whole life has been about making sure that people around me are looked after and have everything they need. I get so much joy from seeing people succeed in whatever it is they are doing. I suppose that is why I always gravitated to jobs in which I could uplift people. Whether that was being a manager at The O2 Arena in London or running accommodation parks on the east coast of Australia with my wife Casey, I have always been drawn to situations that meant I was in a position of support and guidance.

Today, I find myself in a position where I spend my time ensuring that other people are successful. I get a real kick out of working with business owners across the accommodation industry to help them take their businesses from where they are today to even greater success – from delivering new technologies to streamlining business operations, through to helping to put effective complaint-handling processes in place to manage guest feedback.

The accommodation industry is one of the best industries in the world to work in. Our business is literally holidays! We provide a happy and relaxing space for people to spend time building on their relationships with their families and friends. We provide experiences that people look back on with fondness for years to come. The accommodation industry is the stuff of dreams.

For me, working in this industry is about ensuring that my guests have the same experiences that I had when I was growing up. I aim to recreate childhood memories from my own family vacations to make sure that everyone I meet has the same fantastic time that I did. I run my businesses how I want my own holidays to go. I like things to be run smoothly, effectively and with as little impact to my family and friends as possible.

However, anyone familiar with the accommodation industry will tell you that things do not always go according to plan. You will get bad reviews from guests, you will fail to meet their expectations, and you will make mistakes along the way. However, I have learned through trial and error that there are ways you can achieve great things for guests when they come and stay with you, and you can even win guests over with the way you respond to scenarios that impacted them negatively.

That Bad Review

When I started working in the accommodation industry, dealing with feedback from guests was something I expected, but I didn't anticipate how it could affect me. I wasn't prepared for how personally I was going to take the reviews that guests left for my business. I thought that if I put my heart and soul, and my blood, sweat and tears into the running of the business that guests would see that, and they would know I wanted them to have a great time. At the end of the day, though, my dedication and passion didn't make up for situations that didn't go to plan for them. It didn't make up for the delay they had when they checked in. It didn't make up for the scrap of paper that was left in the bin in their room. It didn't make up for the BBQ area that was left dirty by the guests that used it before them.

I quickly realised that I could have all the dedication and passion in the world, but I was still going to get bad reviews. After doing some soul searching, I made the conscious decision that negative criticism from guests was a benefit to me. It meant that someone was taking the time out of their day to tell me that I could run a better business, and all I had to do was listen and deal with the feedback. Since then, I have managed to consistently achieve 4.4/5 stars on Facebook, 9/10 on Booking.com and 4/5 on Tripadvisor.com for my first accommodation business.

My success is something that is easily replicated across any type of service, from cafés to hotels to restaurants. In this book, I am going to break down each element that has led to my success, and give practical and easy steps for you to follow as well.

The Five Phases of a Bad Review

Now that I have sorted out the fundamentals that created the approaches in this book, I can get into what you'll get out of this book, and the first place to start is at its heart: bad reviews.

I believe there are five phases to processing a bad review which I summarise below. Different methodologies are necessary for dealing with each, and I have outlined in detail how you can approach each phase in their own chapters in Part Two of this book.

Phase One: They Said What?!?

In this phase, we come to terms with the fact that people are going to give our businesses feedback – and not all of it will be good. There are different mindsets that sit behind every review your business receives. There are also different types of feedback that can be given to your business. Understanding all of this helps you to deal with reviews in a way that you probably aren't doing today. Sometimes people react negatively when reading criticism about their business; they put it down to the guest being wrong or sweep it under the proverbial rug because they think whatever is being critiscised isn't something that happens very often. In this chapter, you'll learn that ignoring the review is possibly the worst thing you can do.

Phase Two: I'm Crap, You're Crap, We're All Crap

You and I both know how much work goes into running your business, and when you get feedback that someone wasn't happy with what you delivered, you go through a whole raft of emotions. You feel angry, you feel frustrated, you feel sad, and you can even feel like giving up. This phase is critical for all business owners. It allows you to get past yourself to deal with the details behind the review. In this chapter, I'll show you how to get through your emotional reactions to improve your business – and not let them control you.

Phase Three: It's Lies, All Lies!

Phase Three is about recognising when you're justifying the feedback that has been given. 'Oh, it wasn't that bad'; 'It was just a one-off'; 'We dealt with that while they were here, so I don't have to do anything now' – these are all very common thoughts in this phase. It is natural for your mind to justify the feedback and dumb it down. But this is a trap.

The fact is, you can't suit everyone's needs all the time, but no-one has a perfect business. In this chapter, I'll give you practical steps that really work when dealing with bad reviews and online criticism.

Phase Four: Whose Fault is It Anyway?

Phase Four is one of my favourite phases: it involves finding out what went wrong and looking for ways to address the feedback. Not all businesses are created equal, and not all feedback requires a complete overhaul of your business. In this chapter, I will walk through some of the common pieces of feedback that most businesses in the accommodation industry receive and share some practical tips in dealing with them. I also spend some time looking at the types of feedback that aren't your fault and how you should deal with those situations. Hot tip: don't ignore it.

Phase Five: Round Up the Troops, It's Time to Deal

The last phase is where you take action and address the reviews by making the necessary changes and responses. In this chapter, I walk you through the exact process that I use to deal with reviews that have been left for each of my businesses. These methodologies have enabled me to build my businesses to the point where occupancy rates consistently increase annually, and we have a strong and loyal group of guests who return again and again.

Can You Avoid Bad Reviews?

I could have written this entire book based on dealing with and addressing bad reviews; there are plenty of businesses that need help rolling out strategies that will give them the tools to deal with these situations. But remember when I told you I like to be uncomfortable? That I like to jump headlong into situations that allow me to grow as a person and push my businesses to higher reaches? This is where the second half of the book comes into play – and if you're game, it's there waiting for you too.

I firmly believe that you can set up your business in such a way that you can reduce the number of bad reviews you receive to the point that they are insignificant in the overall picture of your business, and you can use those that are left as tools to get more business; you can create such an awesome business that you attract guests that want you to be successful. Using a combination of social media, technology, staff development, compassion and proactivity, you can build a business that stands well above the competitors.

In Part Three, I run through the processes and approaches I use in my own businesses for embracing social media, showing you what works and doesn't work. I also show you how to look at your guests as people in order to build trust that ensures they are loyal and supportive of you and your businesses.

In addition, there are, of course, ways that you can build a team of people around you who deliver quality service that blows your guests out of the water. I will show you how I create and support my team so that my guests are constantly looked after and have the best experiences while staying with us. I will also introduce you to the many ways I use technology to be a leader in the field of customer experience, and how you can encourage true brand ambassadors for your business.

The coming pages will give you the tips and tricks that I have learned over the years in dealing with bad reviews and guests in my own accommodation businesses. I will be sharing my own templates for dealing with guest feedback, both good and bad. I will also be sharing tools that enable my business to stay ahead of guest feedback and avoid negative feedback.

In each chapter, there will be exercises or resources in sections titled – 'A Mini Task for You' or 'A Resource for You' – that will allow you to build an arsenal of tools to take your business to the next level.

Through the rest of the book I have included real feedback that my businesses have been given over the years, and these have been included exactly as received for authenticity.

These methodologies work, and will set up your business to be the best it can be, and help you to provide the best holidays you can for your guests. To take full advantage of these tips and tricks, pull out a piece of paper, open a blank document on your computer or pick up an empty notebook – let's get started.

PART ONE

'LET'S GET STARTED'

CHAPTER 1

The Big, Fat LIE About the Accommodation Industry

*Every time I dealt with front office staff it was as if
they were doing me a favour having me stay in the park.
Requests were commonly met with huffs and sighs.*

~ Rohde

There's something we need to talk about.
Working in the accommodation industry is not like it is on
TV. It's not waking up and going for a surf, watching the sun come
up over the horizon as you float in the ocean with your neighbours
from your quaint seaside town.

It's not walking through perfectly maintained, architecturally
designed grounds, waving to the permanent residents on the way
to your office.

It's not finding a clue to the break-in at the diner the week
before, then leading the chase through the winding hills to catch
the bad guys that live in the next town over.

It's not any of that. It's hard work.

It's long sleepless nights wondering if your occupancy rates are going to cover you for the low season. It's cleaning up after guests who think paying a nightly fee covers dropping their unwanted items wherever they think appropriate. It's unclogging toilet drains at three o'clock in the afternoon because three-year-old Jane flushed a whole toilet roll down the dunny.

On top of all the long, back-breaking hours, of course, there is the feedback you get from guests.

If you're lucky, you get a tonne of fantastic feedback: they loved your facilities, they loved your staff and they had a great holiday. All the work you put in to provide a seamless experience for your guests payed off and the only stressful thing they had to deal with was what time they wanted to hit the pool.

Unfortunately, for most of us working in the accommodation industry, this is not always the case. Sitting among the great feedback are the stinkers, the feedback that has the potential to drive guests away from your business. These little pieces of feedback make your blood run cold and keep you awake at night. They are the dreaded 'bad reviews'.

That's not to say that every bad review your business receives will be on the money. There are many reasons why guests might leave negative reviews, and depending on their motivations you might not need to take their feedback onboard. So let's identify the types of guests whose feedback you can take with a grain of salt.

High-risk Guests and You

How many times have you had to count to three in your head and repeat to yourself the old phrase 'The guest is always right'? This idea is drilled into people working in the tourism and hospitality sector; however, there are times when the business is not at fault for a bad review. There are times when an assumption by the guest is made that leads directly to a bad review. Sometimes it's a miscommunication, and no-one's fault. Sometimes the guest themselves creates their own negative experience.

Not that long ago, when there was a situation that resulted in negative feedback, businesses dealt with guests directly and privately. However, with the increasing popularity of review sites and social media, guest feedback is now available for everyone to see. Despite trying their best to deliver fantastic services to guests, many businesses now live in fear that they will be impacted by a negative review, and, rather than addressing the problem directly they freeze.

The truth is that the customer isn't always right: customers can have an incorrect perception about your business, they can be downright rude, or they could be trying to take advantage of you and your business. There are times when a customer will be totally and utterly wrong. The motivations behind some reviews are usually the nightmares of hardworking business owners. Understanding who these customers are can at least allow you to go back to sleep comfortably.

The Guests Who Fish for a Discount

There are a group of customers who have learned that they can get a discount if only they complain loudly enough. These are the type of customers that cause a scene when something does not go the way they want. They are the customers who will approach you with a hypothetical situation to convince you to discount their stay with you. They are the customers who 'have a lot of friends' who will threaten to leave your business a bad review.

These customers have unfortunately managed to bully their way to a lower price or a free ride time and time again. Your choice as a business owner is to either give in, or not and potentially feel the wrath of the angry customer. A lot of these customers are full of hot air and won't go through with their threats. And even if they do, I am loath to reward their bad behaviour by giving in; this will only encourage them further. A way I test the discount 'fishers' is by offering them a credit to return to our business at a later date. I explain that I would like to show them that if given another chance I am sure that we could provide an experience that exceeds their expectations. You will find that for this type of guest there will be a myriad of excuses for why a credit is not suitable for them. Another telltale sign for me is if they don't give you the opportunity to address their concerns while they are staying with you. If the first I hear about their complaint is after their departure, I am immediately wary. For the ones that follow through, rest assured that your good reviews will balance out any negative criticisms that they may leave for you.

The Guests on a Beer Budget with Champagne Tastes

In your business you offer specific services that are included in the price your guests pay you. Occasionally these services might not align with what your customer expects from your business and this may lead to a bad review. There are a few ways that you can deal with these types of situations. You can make it clear on your website exactly what services are on offer to guests when they come and stay with you. You can highlight your business offerings on social media. You can also take the time to include as much information as possible in your booking confirmation emails about what each of your guests can expect of you and your business. I am a believer in the notion of 'under promise and over deliver'. This will ensure you exceed your guests' expectations.

The more information you give these customers about your business, the better placed you will be to control the reviews these customers are likely to give you. You can dispute their reviews entirely to other readers of review sites by making sure that the information you have listed online is accurate and explicit which can undermine the reviewer's feedback.

The Guests Who Expect the Red Carpet

There are some guests who grace your threshold who expect red-carpet treatment and, for the most part, you will provide this for them. However, there are times when this expectation of you and your team is taken advantage of. There will always be that one guest who expects you to control things that are clearly out of your control – the weather, for example. I am not joking either. I have had a guest ask me to ensure there was sunny weather during their stay, and when there wasn't, left business a 1-star review.

I can understand the guest's point of view: they had taken time away from their busy life to have a holiday but it didn't work out for them. We all work very hard and when we finally manage to get some time off we are disappointed when our perfect holiday doesn't happen the way we imagined. The unfortunate thing is that my business suffers for something that is well and truly out of my control. Getting a bad review for something like the weather is not the biggest issue, I know, but the problem with online review sites is that your overall rating will be affected by something out of your control – and that does suck. But sometimes you do just have to take it on the chin.

The Guests Who Huff and Puff

There are, of course, times when the guest is right. There will be times when your team treats customers poorly. There will also be times when the service that your guests rightly expect fail to be delivered. All good business owners should ensure they always treat guests with respect, but that does not mean you should allow customers to take advantage of you and your business by being dishonest or bullying you and your staff.

There will be times when a guest does not agree with a member of your team. This could be due to a misunderstanding, or it could be a legitimate complaint that your team member is not able to address for that customer at that moment. The best approach here is to listen to both sides of the story and deal with the situation. Making sure you stand up for your team is imperative to their morale. There's no reason that a member of your team should have to deal with abuse or rudeness from a guest. Regardless of who was at fault initially, customers abusing your team should never be tolerated.

These guests will more than likely leave you negative feedback, but you can handle them relatively easy. In later chapters, I'll show you how to respond to these guests and their feedback.

If You Build It, They Will Come

There is an assumption within the holiday industry that if you have a great location for your business, guests will come in droves.

This. Is. Another. Lie.

There is so much more to bringing guests into your business than just having a good location. Just because you have a business next to an awesome beach or right near a highly visited tourist attraction, that is no guarantee that you are going to attract guests.

One of the problems with this attitude is that you are relying solely on things outside your control. What happens when the beach that everyone loves gets trumped by a better beach? What happens when no-one wants to come to that tourist attraction down the road anymore? This will lead to you not having any guests because the one thing you had going for your business is no longer a factor.

If you do not offer a great service to guests in addition to the fantastic location you are lucky to have, then your business won't be ingrained into the minds of your guests and they most likely won't come back. It is much better to have a customer list full of loyal and returning guests than relying exclusively on new clientele.

Some of the best businesses in the accommodation industry don't have the perfect setting. What they do have is the drive and determination to be the best business they can be. They know the exact type of guests they want to attract, and they go after them. They get in the minds of their guest. These businesses are innovative in their approaches, and they make sure they create unique experiences that win loyal guests who then spread the word about how awesome they are.

You Can't Be Everything to Everyone

One thing I want you to stop doing right now is trying to be something that you are not. Don't try to be the guy down the road that runs a similar business to you. Don't try to be a huge hotel chain if you are a small caravan park. Be proud of who you are and what you offer, and have faith in your product. At the end of the day your business is unique to you, and the sooner you embrace this notion, the better you will feel and the better your business will operate.

The one thing that you have that no-one else has is you. No-one will ever approach a situation the same as you. You are your best asset. Being able to look at situations in the cold light of day and being able to see the truth in every scenario will ensure that you are making the best decisions for your business and dealing with feedback in a positive and proactive way.

A Mini Task for You

List five of the top issues that are impacting your business by answering the following questions:

Issue:

Impact:

- What is the likely outcome if left unresolved?
- What steps have you completed to resolve this in the past?
- What worked?
- What didn't work?

If you find this task difficult, then ask guests for some feedback. Ask them what issues they faced when making the decision to come and stay at your business. This list should provide the foundation of your focus as you read and work through the exercises in this book.

CHAPTER 2

What's In It for Me?

Staff friendly enough. You really need to address giving people what they ask for.

- Pat & Mandy

Your customers love you.

Sure, there are a handful of customers each year who come through your business who aren't exactly thrilled with what you've provided them, but most of your customers tell you how much of a great time they had when they stayed with you.

There is absolutely nothing wrong with the service you provide to your customers.

Well, except that one complaint that landed on Facebook that got a heap of comments that you ignored. And there was that email that you just didn't respond to because you were sure that your staff dealt with it.

And there was that other customer who told you they would never come and stay with you again, and you know they won't because you wouldn't if you got that kind of service either.

If we are being honest with each other then I'm sure both you and I can say that there have been times when things could have been handled a lot better than they were. No-one is perfect. Everyone makes mistakes.

I've learned over the years that avoiding problems in my business just leads to stress and anxiety, and creates larger problems than the ones I was trying to avoid in the first place. There is always room for improvement in any business. Keeping your head down and ignoring feedback from your guests is one of the biggest mistakes you can make as a business owner, especially when people are looking online for places to book their holidays and they see reviews that are not that great – and haven't been responded to.

But those are just online reviews, aren't they? You don't need to worry about those, right?

Wrong! These days, feedback from customers can be plastered all over social media, available for everyone who has access to the internet to see and pass judgement on.

According to a report conducted by Bright Local1, in 2017, 97 per cent of consumers read online reviews for local businesses, with 12 per cent looking for a local business online every day. A TripAdvisor survey conducted in 2007 also supported this observation, showing approximately 97.7 per cent of consumers read other travellers' online reviews. Of these, 77.9 per cent of consumers thought online reviews were extremely important or very important for deciding where to stay. That's a lot of people using online reviews to determine if they want to come and stay at your business, and often this can be based on the way you have responded to feedback a previous guest left for you.

It's Not All Bad

The reality is that not everyone who reads a bad review for your business is going to judge you solely on that one situation. Potential guests are people too and they understand that mistakes can happen and that you can't please everyone. The negative criticism that you receive may be completely out of your hands.

When a potential guest is researching your business and deciding if it is the place to stay on their holiday, they will consider the information listed in the review, the tone of the person leaving the review and if the review covers information that is important to them.

If, for example, the review is about a particularly rainy day in the middle of winter and your guest is looking to stay in summer, they will discount the review as it really has no relevance to what they are looking for. And really, most people know business owners aren't responsible for the weather.

Potential guests will also compare and weigh up how many good and bad reviews your business has on the review site. One thing I have learned through managing online reviews is that guests don't believe a business is only getting positive feedback. Yes, it's true you can buy positive reviews, but this is something I encourage you to avoid. Most guests who research your business online are savvy when it comes to review sites and social media, so they know how to spot a fake review.

Don't Take It Too Hard

I haven't always been great at responding to customer feedback. When I first started managing my accommodation business I used to take it hard when someone gave the business a bad review. I would walk around like a black cloud was hanging over me and take it out on those closest to me, and occasionally, the team I worked with.

I would obsess about the details. Why were we at fault? What went wrong? Why would they say that about us?

I just couldn't get the feedback out of my head. I was consumed by the idea that all my hard work, and the time and effort I had put into the business had come to nothing. I would blame myself, convinced that I wasn't managing the business successfully. I would see every new guest as the potential for another piece of negative feedback.

And I was embarrassed. Really embarrassed.

What I started to realise, though, was that getting negative feedback or criticism from guests made my business better. It made my team better. And it made me better. Every time I got bad feedback I was given a little gift. It was highlighting an area of my business that needed improvement. And if I made some small tweaks, I could provide a better service to the next guest who stayed at the park.

Pretty soon I started to look at my business from my guests' eyes, but not from those who returned to the park time and again. Instead, I viewed it from the position of guests who didn't want to come back, and I started to anticipate negative feedback and see areas of my business that could be improved.

There's No Truth to It Anyway

Looking critically at your business is not easy. The first reaction you have when someone leaves you negative feedback is that it couldn't have been as bad as what they said it was. Surely the experience they had was blown out of proportion. I know my staff aren't rude to my guests. I know that we have the right processes in place for guests to contact us outside of office hours …

The reality is, the feedback left is from your guest's perspective; it's their truth. This is why it is important that you find out what really happened and not just brush it off. Getting to the truth may reveal an exaggeration, something that has been blown out of proportion. But how will you know that's the case unless you find out what really happened?

You can't be everywhere in your business at all times, and not everyone works to their best every day either. But a complaint needs to be investigated and not simply brushed off as something that a guest did or didn't do. It could be that your staff were rude to a guest. It could be that your guest had a terrible experience that was a direct result of the service your business provided them. For the most part, a guest will leave feedback for you to improve the experience they had for future guests. This is a gift: free advice that you can use to improve your business offerings.

Knowing Where Fault Lies

It can be simple to blame a guest for something that didn't go according to plan. They just didn't understand the type of booking that they made. They clearly didn't read the email that explained our check-in process and how our deposit system works. Alternatively, it's just as simple to blame the receptionist who was looking after the front office that morning.

That would be easy, wouldn't it? Then there would be nothing you would need to do to change the way you run the business. Because it's not really your fault.

If only that were true.

And then there are the instances of miscommunication. Most of the negative reviews or situations that I deal with in my business come down to a miscommunication. From something simple like a guest not knowing where to park their car, through to staff missing specific requirements that a guest outlined on their booking.

Once you have gotten to the bottom of the feedback and you know what led to it, you can decide what to do next. Breaking down the feedback allows you to view each aspect of that specific situation and see where processes can be improved in the running of your business.

There might not be anything that could be done to avoid the exact situation happening again, but there could be ways you can improve in other areas: for example, you might decide there is nothing you need to do other than respectfully respond to the guest with the facts of the situation and leave it at that.

The only way that you can turn negative feedback provided by guests into a positive for your business and work on addressing the problem is knowing where the fault of that situation lies.

The Benefit of Feedback

Nobody wants to receive negative criticism. Having your Facebook or TripAdvisor page littered with feedback that paints you in a bad light is something that keeps you up at night. But negative feedback isn't always that bad for you.

How you respond allows you to demonstrate to your potential guests how passionate you are about your business and the feedback that you receive from people who stay with you.

Even if the feedback is untrue, a potential guest is looking at the way you conduct yourself and respond, just as much as the amount of negative feedback left for your business. I know you might not want to play the guest's game and would rather not respond. But anyone reading that complaint about your business knows nothing except what is written. They weren't there when it happened. They have no idea if the information listed is true or if it isn't. If it's untrue, by responding in a way that provides the facts of the situation you can win fans and potential guests while expanding on the context behind the complaint.

If there is a sense of truth to negative feedback that has been left for you, a well worded response gives you the opportunity to demonstrate that even when things don't go to plan, you are able to admit your faults and improve. Think about it. Would you choose to stay, or do business with, someone who gives the impression that everything is always perfect? Or would you prefer to deal with someone who realises that things can go awry at times, and when they do, they are dealt with in a professional manner with the problem not ignored, denied or swept under the rug?

The beauty of online feedback is that it doesn't matter if you were at fault because you can win the situation unfolding online. What matters to people thinking about staying at your business is that you took the time to respond. You can demonstrate that you show gratitude and respect to people, even if they are being unfair and overly critical of you and your business.

Being responsive to customers and making sure you have processes in place to deal with complaints is a crucial element in running a business. It is the best way to measure your success, ensuring, that you can win clients and improve your revenue year after year. There will always be someone critical of your business and what you offer. Knowing how to filter out the noise and get to the bottom of situations, and understanding that it is okay to fail, is critical when dealing with bad reviews.

The reality is that you will never be able to please everyone, and there will be situations that are out of your control. You are far better off making changes and improvements based on genuine feedback, and putting your time and effort into the situations you can control.

CHAPTER 3

How to Thrive and Survive Today
and Every Day

*Unfortunately we only stayed for 1 night but were
most impressed by everything & will stay longer next time.*
~ Roslyn

Having your customers tell you what is wrong with your
business is awesome.

No, really, it is!

Getting negative feedback is a great way to improve your business. It can highlight where your processes don't really work, and it can give you an insight into what guests are looking for that you don't already have in place.

There are two types of businesses that exist: those that have already had a bad review, and those that haven't … yet. It is impossible to run a business today and not collect a bad review, but if you are lucky enough to not have had one, you either have a business that is brand new or you haven't managed to locate that review. Believe me, it's out there.

But I'll tell you a secret. There is a third type of business. It's the business that goes under the radar. The one that is in touch with the best of technology, has killer processes and builds a tremendous team to interact with guests.

Ladies and gentlemen, I introduce you to: the businesses that *avoid* bad reviews.

'Impossible!' I hear you say. 'No-one can avoid bad reviews. No-one can provide the best of everything to every guest.'

Well that is true, so there is a caveat. What we are talking about are the businesses that avoid genuine negative feedback. After all, your business is going to receive criticism for things that are out of your control. Your business may be blamed for being too far away from the beach, or it might even be blamed for the birds singing to each other at six o'clock in the morning.

Those elements are something that you have little ability to control, and if you try you will spend the rest of your days cursing the birds.

Now that we have this secret out in the open, I bet you're wondering how to go about setting up your business to be one that avoids bad reviews. Well, let me tell you.

Social Media is Your Friend

I am still surprised at how many businesses there are in the accommodation industry that don't utilise social media to its fullest potential. Being online is one of the best ways to avoid receiving negative reviews from guests. It also gives the opportunity to reach out to a whole group of potential guests that you otherwise might not have been able to access.

Social media gives you multiple options to avoid bad reviews, you just need to be a little bit creative with it. One of the simplest ways to avoid bad reviews is just by having a presence on a specific website.

Most people don't like conflict, they will avoid it as much as possible. However social media gives guests who wouldn't normally complain an avenue to do just that. By being active on social media you can dissuade some guests from leaving a review, because they're more likely to be aware that you are going to read it – and potentially take them to task by responding to it. While this won't address their concerns, it will allow you to avoid the review hitting an open forum.

See Your Guests as People, Not Dollars

For most of us, guests who come to our business are there for a one-off stay. We likely won't ever see them again. But if they are not treated properly, this can impact your business for years to come.

Everyone who comes to your business is unique. Each guest is important and everything they need is something that you need to address. While this sounds impossible, it's not. Treating your guests with respect and dignity is something that most businesses do. But building trust with a guest is something that is a little harder.

So how do you make sure these guests connect with you quickly and trust that you are delivering what they need? Simple. You treat them like they are people. One of the easiest ways to build trust with someone quickly is just by remembering their name. It's not that hard to do. Your guest knows you see dozens of people in any given day, but the fact that you remember their name makes them feel that you see them, they are memorable, and you are not just looking at them as dollars to fill your bank account.

Another way to build trust is to slow down. Yes, you heard

right, just SLOW DOWN. In a study conducted in the 1970s called 'Jerusalem to Jericho', the premise of which was based on the story of the Good Samaritan, Princeton psychologists John Darley and Daniel Batson concluded that a person not in a hurry may stop and offer help to a person in distress, while a person in a hurry is more likely to keep going. I think this translates to our ability to build trust with people, not just helping those in distress. If you are pressed for time in a high-pressure environment – like the reception area of your business – you are far less likely to present as someone who is trustworthy and empathic. My staff know how important it is to slow down and take the time to truly listen to our guests during the check-in process, even if there is a queue out the door.

Take Control of Your Reviews

No-one said you had to wait until after a guest leaves to get a review from them, did they? Did that just blow your mind a little? We introduced mid-stay reviews to our parks a while back and we have seen a massive change in both our positive reviews and interactions with our guests.

You don't have to be formal about it either. Simply taking a walk around the park at intervals during your guest's stay can show you care and that you're open to hearing ways to improve their stay *while they are still there*. Plus this means you can avoid getting a nasty surprise when they leave.

The more visible you and your team are, the more you will reduce the amount of bad reviews and create a personal bond with your guests that I can guarantee can't be replicated by your competitors – because they're not you.

Build a Great Team

I bet you already have a great team, right? I mean, you wouldn't be running a successful business if the people who worked with you weren't doing their jobs. But do your guests know who they are, or do they only know you? Can your team do what they need to do daily without asking you for something? Feeling a little unsure now?

Building a great team is more than having a group of people who know how to do their jobs well. It's also about empowering your employees to make decisions. It's about knowing them beyond the work environment.

But how does this help your business avoid bad reviews?

As much as you like to think you have the answers to everything, you don't. You also can't be in multiple places at the same time. By having a great team that can look out for potential problems or suggest different approaches to issues, you create a better business which leads to you providing a level of service beyond guest expectations. The better your business is at operating, the better it is at avoiding situations that let guests down.

Embrace Technology

The digital world is amazing; there are new technologies being developed every day. Your business can take full advantage of these technologies to create a seamless experience for your guests, also ensuring that you avoid as many bad reviews as possible.

There are fantastic systems available that can automate guest bookings and check-in processes, allowing your team to deal with the more personal aspects, like welcoming your guests. Technology can also show you via email tracking which guests have opened their confirmation email, when they opened them and how many times they have read them. This allows you to highlight to your reception team which guests might not be aware of your park policies and facilities, so that your guests can then be informed at check-in.

It's also possible to incorporate an SMS automation with your booking system to send out notifications to your guests that cover anything from surf and weather reports to special offers. Before your guests arrive, you can show them your facilities via virtual tours detailing exactly what is available and where to find things like toilets and showers.

Most bad reviews stem from miscommunications or incorrect expectations of your business. Using technology, you can provide more information to your guests before they arrive, allowing them to develop realistic expectations that help you to avoid bad reviews.

Build a Solid Backbone

Any business owner who has a slightly successful business will tell you there must be processes. Your team needs to know how to welcome a guest to the park. You need to know how you're going to get a guest from point A to point B. And you need to know how and when you are going to clean the facilities at your park. But most importantly, you need to know how you're going to get paid.

Processes are the central nervous system of a business; they ensure that your day-to-day tasks get done correctly and ensure smooth experiences for everyone involved – from your team to your guests. And the way that you set up your processes can ensure that your business avoids bad reviews.

Your guests will get the best level of service they can from your business if you take the time to think about what a great experience is for your guest. If you know what the gold standard is, you can then put processes in place so that everything your team does and everything that you do ensures this experience is delivered.

If you do this, not only will you avoid bad reviews, but you will also create a business that people will want to return to.

Becoming a business that is set up to avoid bad reviews is not an impossible or expensive task. The keys are treating people with respect and listening to what your guests and team are telling you about your business and acting on it.

The reality is, of course, that you won't be able to please everyone; your business will attract people who thought they were getting something that you weren't able to deliver. Your guests will compare your business with another business that isn't the same because it has different options and facilities to yours. There will always be those guests who don't read or listen to the details no matter how many times you try to inform them.

There is always going to be something that happens that is out of your control. What you can control, however, is how you deal with each situation. You can choose to deal with people with respect, and demonstrate to your guests that you are prepared to act on their feedback. You can choose to empower your staff to take ownership of decisions that help the business to operate success-fully and offer a service to your guests that you would like to buy. You can choose to build a business that makes you proud.

PART TWO

THE FIVE
PHASES OF A
BAD REVIEW

CHAPTER 4

There's Something You Should Know

THE REARRANGING OF THE BINS AT 6AM WAS A BIT MUCH.
~ Geoff

A re you ready for an ugly truth?
People are talking about your business negatively right now. They are doing it with their neighbours, they are doing it with their family.

They are even doing it in front of millions of people.

And the kick in the guts?

They don't need your permission to do it.

Reviews of your business are as readily available as opinions. And just like opinions, they can be wrong, they can be misinformed and they can be close to the truth.

Today, especially with the abundance of review sites available online, we live in a world where sharing your opinion is celebrated. From the best coffees in Melbourne to the worst accommodation to stay at on the Gold Coast.

And people LOVE reviews.

Did you know that TripAdvisor has such a huge influence on

tourism that negative reviews can impact the tourism revenue of entire countries? Not hotels. Not tourist destinations. COUNTRIES.[2]

The trust that people place in reviews on websites like TripAdvisor means that reviews have a lot of weight. Ignorance is not an option; you have to take control.

'But I didn't set up profiles for my business on review sites,' I hear you say.

Unfortunately, it doesn't work that way. Anyone who is a member of a review site can set up a profile for your business, and they don't need your permission to do it. That's how the sites work: they're set up for the reviewer and future readers of the review, not for the businesses the review is about.

Before we get too far ahead of ourselves, I think it's worthwhile defining a good review and a bad review, and how we measure these. I'll also look at where to find the bad reviews, how the top five review sites work, and the reasons behind why you might be avoiding checking your reviews and responding to them.

How to Tell the Good from the Bad

In my businesses, we measure the success and failure of our guests' stays with a post-stay survey (and other feedback results) through a system known as Net Promoter Score. But what exactly is it? The Net Promoter Score (NPS) is a guest loyalty metric that was created by Fred Reichheld, Bain & Company and Satmetrix in 2003. It is based on the perspective that every company's customers can be one of three types: Promoter, Passive or Detractor.

A 'Promoter' guest is enthusiastic and loyal. They continually buy from the company and 'promote' the company to their friends and family. These guests return to your business again and again and always go the extra mile in promoting your business. They often know your name and, in some cases, they will come to your business's defence if negative feedback appears online.

A 'Passive' guest is happy with what they experienced but can easily be tempted to go elsewhere with an attractive competitor deal. Passive guests may become Promoters if you improve your product, service or guest experience. These guests may only slightly engage with you during their stay, or are there for a few nights and might not return. Online, this type may like your Facebook page and some of your posts, but typically they don't share content or interact.

Finally, the 'Detractor' guest is unhappy, feels mistreated and their experience will generally mean they won't return. Detractor guests also have an increased likelihood of switching to a competitor, as well as warning potential guests to stay away from your company. There are varying degrees of detractor types, from a guest who simply won't return, through to one who will go out of their way to ensure others don't stay at your business. Online, this type will leave negative reviews (sometimes across multiple sites) and will possibly engage negatively with others' positive feedback across social media.

Assigning Ratings to Your Guests

'On a scale of 0 to 10 how likely are you to recommend us to a friend or colleague?' This is the key question in order to obtain your NPS score. Guests who give you a rating of 9 or 10 are considered Promoters. Guests who give you a rating of 7 or 8 are Passive guests and, while they are not dissatisfied, they do not factor into the NPS. Lastly, any guests who provide you a rating of 6 or lower are considered your Detractors.

The NPS model is a reliable scale to determine a good, moderate and bad review. Another common scoring method exists and it is one that should be familiar to people in the accommodation industry: the 1–5-star review system. This model is used across most review sites, including Facebook, Google and TripAdvisor.

'But do the Promoter, Passive and Detractor guests fit into this star-rating model?' I'm glad you asked.

Top guest ratings sit up around the 4.5–5-star reviews: this group are likened to Promoters.

In the middle on 3.5–4-star reviews are Passive guests. Lastly 1–3-star reviews are for Detractors.

To sum up:

- good reviews from Promoters: 4.5–5-stars and NPS 9–10
- middle reviews from Passives: 3.5–4-stars and NPS 7–8
- bad reviews from Detractors: 1–3-stars and NPS 1–6.

Where are Our Reviews Hanging Out?

As I mentioned earlier, there are a tonne of review sites available to your guests. So how do you know where to go to find what's waiting for you? The sheer volume of review sites to check is an intimidating task, and it can make you want to pretend the whole mess doesn't exist.

My approach is to go where the majority of my guest bookings are and make sure I have those areas under control. Your booking system should indicate where your online bookings are coming from; this is where you should make sure you have your best game face on.

It also pays to have a presence in the most common or popular sites that people visit to look for reviews. I've made a top five list of the sites I recommend your business manages: TripAdvisor, Booking.com, Facebook, Google and Expedia. There are a number of other sites that may be relevant for your business, so you may just need to get on your favourite search engine and see what pops up.

TripAdvisor

TripAdvisor is currently the number-one review site for the accommodation industry, so paying attention to this site is a must to ensure you have control over the reviews that are left for you. You need to put your best digital face forward on TripAdvisor by ensuring you respond to reviews calmly and never leave reviews without a response (even the good ones). Guests can even make bookings directly on TripAdvisor which means having control of your property on the site a priority.

TripAdvisor also moderates reviews by giving them merit ratings, so pretty much everyone is encouraged to be a professional reviewer.

Booking.com

This site is another big hitter in the accommodation review space. It boasts approximately 1,500,000 properties, and over 123,000 destinations in 229 countries and territories – that's a stack of businesses that guests can leave reviews for. Like TripAdvisor, guests can book directly from the website, meaning they can research and make decisions all in one place.

Facebook

As of the third quarter of 2017 over 2.07 billion active users were plugged in to this social media giant, so having a profile on Facebook, and actively using it, and managing feedback and reviews is important for any business that operates today. People are already using this platform to share in almost every aspect of their day, so leaving reviews is the next logical step. Facebook also has the added advantage of being free advertising for you (remember those Promoters we talked about?), but we will discuss this later in the book.

Google Maps

Never underestimate the website that is used by more people on the internet than any other. Google Maps might be impacting your business without you even realising it. Lists of reviews are available when searching on specific businesses or destinations with Google Maps; people can also easily write reviews or give a star-rating if signed in. Being on Google Maps and managing your reviews here also gives you the added advantage of a boost in local search engine optimisation (SEO) – part of the algorithms Google uses to provide search results – so it makes great business sense to have a presence and a healthy number of stars on this site.

Expedia

Expedia is another on the forefront of review and booking sites for accommodation. Founded in 1996 by Microsoft, it now stands on its own outside of the technology powerhouse. The simple 5-star system, internal rating rewards and cheap last-minute booking feature makes it attractive for guests to jump on and read about or review your business.

If I Ignore It, It Will Just Go Away

Knowing that people are leaving you feedback and where to find it is just part of what you need to know when taking steps to manage reviews. Social media and review sites are like sharp swords: they can cut both ways. You open yourself up to the good reviews and feedback from guests that loved staying with you, but then there are the bad reviews – the ones you wish would just go away.

Ignoring reviews is something I discourage you from doing for two main reasons. One: you have been given an insight into an area of your business that didn't work for a guest, so you can make it better. Two: this is your opportunity to show potential guests that you take the time to respond and deal with issues raised.

There will be times when someone leaves vague feedback about *something* that *kind of* happened and they *sort of* didn't like it and *yeah* ... You might read on blogs or in articles on business websites that it is okay to ignore this type of feedback. I'm going to tell you that you shouldn't. Not everyone is great at writing, and some people are scared that they might offend you. There might be nothing to the complaint at all other than a general feeling that they didn't like what they experienced. However, if you take the time to respond and ask questions about this kind of review, you will show not only the reviewer but also everyone else that you care about their feedback. Never ignore an opportunity to engage with a guest – potential, current or previous.

Just like ignoring feedback when it's vague, there is a common perception that you should also ignore feedback that comes from only one person. But just because it's only one review, doesn't mean you shouldn't address it. It might only be a single event that was out of your control, but the fact the guest took the time to send you feedback needs to be taken into account. Especially when you consider a recent study that showed that for every person who complained, there were up to 26 people who also felt the same way.[3]

Remember that as soon as someone gives you online feedback, it is now available to everyone who views the site. Always have the approach that there are thousands of people awaiting your response – not just the person who left the comment for you.

A Mini Task for You

Find and make a list of the most important sites where your business is listed using the following strategies:

- Perform a Google search on your business name. This should bring up a number of sites where your business name appears.

- Check the booking sources in your booking system to identify popular online travel agents.

- Log on to social media platforms such as Facebook and perform a search for your business name.

- Make note of how many reviews have been left on each of these sites.

Once you have a comprehensive list, find the top five sites based on the number of reviews that have been left. Feel free to include more than five if you feel that the number of reviews warrants your attention. Calculate your current average number of stars on each site, and use these results to calculate an average overall score. Use this score as an indication as to how your business is performing. Check your average score every month. The initial score is less important than the way the score is trending. Of course a higher score is better, but if your score is trending upwards then that is a good sign that your business is producing satisfied customers. If your score is trending downwards then you need to take action. Read on to see how you can improve this trend.

CHAPTER 5

Phase One – They Said What!?!

The pillows smelt of sweat, I purchased some from Target, maybe pillow protectors so they can be washed after each guest leaves.

~ *Donna*

Understanding who your guests are sets you up for success. I mean, if you don't know who you are going to target, then how do you make decisions about how your business runs?

You don't know who to market to.

You don't know what to offer.

You don't even know where to focus your advertising.

The same can be said for people who leave you reviews. If you don't understand people's motivations for leaving reviews, then it's hard to work out the best way to respond to them.

People leave reviews for a whole range of reasons. Some are about your business and how you conduct yourself. Some are about the experience the guest had, good or bad. Some are for social interaction, simply a way to engage with other like-minded people.

A whole culture and community has sprung up around reviewing products and services, some sites even have rewards or status based on their members leaving reviews. Understanding this community's motivations helps to formulate your strategy in dealing with reviews for your business.

The Seven Types of Guests Who Leave Reviews

During the time that I have been managing accommodation businesses, I have come to believe that there are seven types of guests who leave reviews: the Grateful Guest, the Neglected Guest, the So-so Guest, the Firecracker Guest, the Disorganised Guest, the By-the-book Guest and the 1%-er Guest. While everyone doesn't fit neatly into a nice little box, I have dealt with countless guests, happy and mad, and can usually spot the different types of guests a mile off.

The Grateful Guest

Starting out in a positive place, let me introduce you to the Grateful Guest. This person typically engages with you during their stay; they always have a smile and a wave ready for your staff. The Grateful Guest will usually include specific team members' names in their feedback and will always be happy to return to your accommodation. They can be either a Promoter or Passive on NPS and will leave 4–5-star reviews like:

> *'Thank you so much for our family vacation, will be back for sure.'*

> *'The staff were amazing, couldn't have asked for more.'*

> *'Julie on your reception needs a raise. She's such a lovely young girl.'*

The Neglected Guest

The Neglected Guest is usually the person who had a negative experience and didn't feel that you addressed their concerns or issues while they stayed with you. Their problem usually is not major, though, and the experience didn't impact too much on their stay with you. These people fall into the Passive or 3-star group of reviewers but can also be Detractors, rating a 6 on the NPS. Typical comments from this group include:

'The rooms were neat and tidy, but the check-in process was a little long.'

'The rooms were of a good size, however we needed fresh towels and didn't get any when we asked.'

'Good location, good facilities, staff friendly, asked for sauce with my chips but it didn't come.'

The So-so Guest

The So-so Guest is generally someone who had a decent experience of your business but didn't feel that you provided them with anything other than what was expected. This guest is usually the one that you only see at check-in and check-out and, in my experience, they usually have a young family or are one of a pair of travelling grey nomads. This guest also falls into the 3-star category and will be a Detractor on the NPS (normally scoring a 6). Typical comments from this group include:

'Lovely location, park was easy to navigate, dog friendly.'

'The pool was good, parking was easy.'

'The rooms look like they could do with a freshen up, but otherwise good for a quick stop.'

The Firecracker Guest

The Firecracker is typically the guest who has very high expectations of your business before they even get there. This guest is impatient with any delays that impact their stay, from questions asked at check-in through to how far away the facilities are from their room. This guest will fall into the 2-star spot and will be a Detractor on the NPS, scoring 3–6. Typical feedback includes:

'Did not know that the business required a deposit, this was not clear on booking.'

'The park was good, however staff could do with improving their attitudes.'

'Asked for a double bed, got two singles pushed together instead. Room was close to pool.'

The Disorganised Guest

The Disorganised Guest is self-explanatory. They are the ones who haven't read the information about your business or any emails that you send them. They also don't read information on-site, no matter how big and red the sign is. Despite being so disorganised, this category of guest will normally leave a lot of information in a review and can become easily embarrassed, which means they can leave you a good review or a bad one. This guest is all over the stars and the Net Promoter Score, depending on how you handle them. Typical feedback from the Disorganised Guest includes:

'The rooms were great, but we were not aware we could not bring our own food.'

'The manager was very rude to me and my family even after I explained I did not get their emails.'

'Good location but will not return. They did not have big enough sites available for our caravan. They said that they offer sizes on booking, but this was not clear.'

The By-the-book Guest

The By-the-book Guest is a guest who has high expectations of your business before arriving. This guest can range from Promoter to Detractor on the NPS, scoring 1–10 and will leave you 1–5-star reviews. This guest takes everything into account, from something in your control like booking procedures, to something not in your control like the weather. This guest has normally spent a long time planning their vacation, and will raise any issue with you as soon as it happens, so you come to know them well. This guest is watching and rating from their first engagement with your business. Typical feedback comments are:

'The stay was pleasant enough, however we would have liked more options for our family when it rained.'

'Our holiday was amazing. We enjoyed the beach that was near and the staff were always very helpful to us whenever we had questions.'

'We will not stay here again. My son was stung by a bee and when we went to the office for assistance they only offered medical aid but did not move us from our camping spot or offer a discount.'

The 1%-er Guest

The last guest I wanted to talk about is the one that will more than likely haunt you, and is the one you really won't be able to do anything about. They can fall into any of the above types and their feedback will range from positive to negative. These guests are the ones that have been impacted by something that has nothing to do with your business; you just happened to be at the receiving end of their complaint that day. They can also be guests that, no matter what you do, will never be satisfied as they are determined to find fault. It will take practice to spot the 1%-er, and when you do the best course of action is to deal with the scenario that brought them across your path and try to let it go as best you can.

While guests can span all ages, races and genders, identifying them as one of these seven types as they come through your door can help you in heading off any negative feedback before it hits the internet or your internal rating systems. The better you understand the guest and what is driving them, the more easily you can provide them with a great experience while they stay with you. Putting people into categories can help you formulate responses; however, everyone is unique and the way they behave will be based on the way they are treated. Never think that you can't win someone over or change their mind simply because you think 'Oh, they are one of *those* guests'. Challenge yourself to deliver the best to them and you will relish the results.

Why Did You Say That?

While understanding the type of guests responsible for reviews is a great step in managing guest experiences, understanding *why* people leave these reviews can help you to deal with these reviews online. Not everyone who leaves a review wants to attack your business. As a matter of fact, I find that a bad review is usually not about revenge at all. There are usually five motivators behind why someone leaves a review for your business.

Sharing is Caring

People often write reviews for selfless reasons: because they want to share their experience with other people. If a guest has had a fantastic time, they want to ensure that anyone who is thinking about staying with you knows this. Likewise, if someone has had a bad experience, they want to make sure that people are aware of the problems. These reviews are often given in detail and can be filled with enthusiasm and praise if positive, or warnings and doom if negative.

Saying Thank You

The best motivator behind leaving reviews is because people want to say thank you for the service they received. This motivator is different from Sharing is Caring as feedback is less detailed and will typically either be a simple thank you or a high rating. These reviewers will return to your business and be your most loyal guests. They will also tend to get involved with your social media account, coming to your defence if negative feedback is given by pointing out that they have not had the same negative experience.

They Want You to Be Better

Even if someone has had a negative experience, they can be motivated to leave reviews because they want your business to be better for the next person. This kind of review is typically balanced with good and bad attributes, making it a reasonable piece of feedback. These reviewers will always offer criticism along with suggestions on how to improve. While these are bad reviews overall, they can be helpful, enabling you to take action to address their concerns for future guests.

They Want to Be Heard

Everyone has an opinion on something, and, for the most part, people just want to be heard. These reviewers are motivated by the desire to have someone, somewhere, listen to what they have to say. This can be someone who has raised a complaint but felt that their concern was not addressed. Alternatively, it can be a group of guests, or someone holidaying with a group, who may have a negative experience but didn't want to raise their feedback while in the group. Or they can be someone who didn't have a concern at all, but still wants their experience recognised and validated. This motivator can drive people to leave either good or bad reviews, depending on the situation they experienced.

They Want to Join the Gang

Review platforms have become a way for people to connect with each other through a shared loved of holiday destinations and experiences. They have become a social network enabling people to receive a confidence boost and connection by leaving reviews which other like-minded people can comment on. These reviewers are socially motivated and typically spend a lot of time online. They are usually people who build strong networks of friends on sites like Facebook or Twitter, and they become known as people who can be relied on for reviews of destinations or businesses within the accommodation industry. Some of these people may even have Facebook groups specialising in certain destinations. The people motivated in this way can either be an active Promoter of your business or a Detractor dedicated to driving people away.

A Mini Task for You

Now that you have found the sites where your business is listed online, it's time to start looking at the feedback that has been left for you.

Pick one site and sort the ratings so that only 1-2-star feedback is shown.

If you can't find enough low-rated feedback on one website, compile feedback from a few other websites, so that you have at least five or six pieces.

Read the feedback and see if you can find a pattern.

If you can't, that's okay, but make a list of the main problems so you can identify what your business needs to address.

CHAPTER 6

Phase Two – I'm Crap, You're Crap, We're All Crap

Leaking showers, wet floor. Noise of construction of grassed areas. Public walking through. Early morning joggers making noise at 5am. Little activity for older children.

~ Mr Creeman

Have you ever had one of those dreams where you just can't seem to get anything right?

Anytime you talk to someone they're angry at you, for no apparent reason.

Or the dream where you try to help someone, and it just gets worse?

Ever had this dream while you're completely awake?

There are days when you get to work and all you get is complaint after complaint.

You open your computer and there is a wall of emails that is just one negative item after another. You open your Facebook and a complaint has hit the page and, as you watch, the post gets more likes than any other post for that month.

There are days when you wish you could turn around, go back home, jump under the covers and stay there.

People are just mean.

They don't understand the work you put in to making sure your business runs smoothly. Mrs Joe Blogs didn't know that you were up until 4 am with a teething kid and that's why you got angry at her when she complained about needing extra towels for the fifth time.

Guests don't think that you know the faults in your business, but you know them better than anyone.

Can't they just focus on the positive and not the negative?

Can't they just give you a break!?

The facts are, no they can't, and no they won't. Your guests have paid to stay with you and expect a certain level of service. And you are going to hear about it, one way or another, when things don't go according to plan.

And it is totally okay for you to be despondent and, well, plain angry when criticism comes pouring in.

Feeling the Burn of Negativity

Human beings are wonderfully complex and emotional animals, and engaging with other humans is going to put you through a roller-coaster of emotions. Unfortunately, the good emotions won't be in play all the time. When you get feedback that you aren't expecting (or maybe you are) it is going to set you off down a path of negative emotions.

It's easy to manage your day-to-day workload when you're feeling happy and excited, and things are all 'kumbaya' by the fire, and everyone is laughing and holding hands. The real test of your business-running capabilities is when it's all doom and gloom and there is a queue of unhappy guests with pitchforks ready to throw you on the fire.

When I opened a negative review, or if I got one in person, it used to set me off on a path of negative thoughts and feelings that made me create more negative scenarios in my business. Depending on the situation, I would feel: frustrated and irritated, worried and nervous, angry and aggravated, rejected or inadequate. Over time I found ways to face these emotions, work through the struggles, and deal with the criticisms. Knowing why you feel a certain way and what you can do to overcome the situation, and seeing your guest's perspective can help you deal with these situations easily and effectively. Below, I outline the ways you can deal with these emotions.

Frustration and Irritation

You put a lot of hard work and effort into your business and when things don't go right, it is common to feel frustrated and irritated. This typically comes about when you feel that you are trapped or stuck in some way and can't find a way forward. For example, you may have received feedback from a guest about your facilities that you already know needs to be addressed, but financially you're not able to address them.

Take a Step Back

The How: The best way to deal with frustration and irritation is to stop and evaluate the situation and ask: what exactly is making you frustrated? Writing this down can help you to focus your thoughts. To counteract the negative emotions, think of something positive. For example, the negative feedback may be on your business's check-out process; the positive aspect could be your guest suggests how to improve your services.

The Why: Thinking about the situation that made you feel frustrated in a positive way flips your thought process. It forces you to focus on something other than the feeling of frustration. When you put yourself into a positive headspace it will help you approach the scenario in a proactive way.

Worry and Nervousness

Running a business means you tend to focus with laser precision on your bottom line; you know within a cent how much money you are making and how much more you need to make. Worrying about anything that has the potential to impact your bottom line is completely rational. Let's face it – it does take a lot of effort to see a bad review as a positive for your business. The first thoughts you are likely to have are along the lines of 'I hope this doesn't stop people staying here'. Being in this mindset can lead you to avoid bad reviews and hope they go away. But knowing how to address these thoughts and rising above them will ensure you don't make those negative thoughts come true.

Remove Yourself

The How: When I feel nervous or worried about feedback, I physically remove myself from the situation. I do this by taking a walk out of the park, going for a drive or spending some time with my kids or wife.

The Why: Removing yourself from the negative space can help to give you perspective. Focusing on the positive things that come out of your business, like your family's welfare, can flip your mind towards a healthier way of thinking and alleviate your concerns so you can look at the situation from a fresh perspective.

Anger and Aggravation

When things don't go right, you can see red. If you get a review from a guest and you can clearly see what went wrong and why, it is normal to get angry. You could also be in a situation where you dealt with a guest's concern at the time it occurred, but they still went and splashed it all over TripAdvisor and Facebook.

Anger is one of those emotions that most people don't handle very well, and dealing with a situation while angry can make matters worse. When I first started addressing feedback from guests, I used to get incredibly angry and then felt shitty about myself, so I learned as a result to take another simple approach and embrace this emotion instead.

Embrace the Hulk

The How: When you feel yourself getting angry, stop what you are doing right away. Don't read any more of that review. Open a blank document on your computer or grab a piece of paper and a pen and write a response. Write it as angry as you want it to be. Use an F-bomb every second word. Go to town on that guest. Tell them how much you hated them staying at your business, tell them how wrong they are. Take all that anger and put it into that response. When you are done, delete it.

The Why: Anger is like an overfilled beanbag. It wants to burst. It wants to escape into the world and fill it with little angry beans of Styrofoam. Holding onto anger can make you sick; it can affect you physically and it can impact everyone around you.There is nothing wrong with getting that feeling out of your body. When you do, you can deal with the situation in a far better way – and I have learned that letting go of the anger allows me to see the situation from a fresh perspective (while sometimes eating a little bit of humble pie along the way).

Rejection

Your business has a lot of you in it, and the reality is that everything on offer is something you've created. You make all the decisions that ultimately lead to what your guests experience. When it doesn't come off the way you want it to, it can be like someone just slapped you in the face. When a guest does not like particular services or facilities, business owners commonly feel rejected. Deep down we want to be liked, because being liked means more people will want to come and stay with us.

Assess Yourself

The How: If you're feeling rejected by a guest, the best way to handle it is by tackling that situation head-on. Think about the situation from the guest's perspective and make a list of five ways the situation could have been managed differently. This will enable you to see where you could turn that feeling of rejection into a list of possible accomplishments. This list can also be the outline of your response to the guest. Bonus!

The Why: Thinking about the situation from the guest's perspective will put you in their mindset. Thinking about it from an abstract point of view can help you separate yourself from the situation. When a guest provides feedback via a bad review, they aren't thinking about *you* personally (even if they call you out specifically). They are thinking about how it impacted *them*. You, in all honesty, are not a factor in their thoughts.

Feeling Inadequate

Welcome to the club of business owners who feel inadequate in their business after reading a bad review. Group membership: everyone who has received a bad review from a guest. There is a feeling of failure that runs through every business owner. You can rest assured that at some stage even the owners of the Hilton have lain awake at night concerned about bad reviews of their business. Feelings of inadequacy are completely normal. You are your own worst critic, and when a guest calls you out with a bad review this feeling can bubble to the surface and easily take over your thoughts. But you can win against this negative emotion.

You Have the Skills

The How: You know your business better than anyone; you are the fount of all knowledge. When you feel inadequate, just think about all the things you do in a day. Think about your team and how much they rely on you to help them with their jobs. Think about all the positive reviews you have received and all the great interactions you have with guests on an hourly basis. Then tell me you feel inadequate. I bet you can't!

The Why: Taking a step back from this emotion and reminding yourself of everything you have achieved will give you the kick up the arse that you need. Wallowing in this emotion will only turn your negative thoughts into actions. The more you think you are inadequate to deal with the situation, the more inadequate you will be.

The emotional cycle that comes with bad reviews is normal. No-one likes to deal with something negative, but taking the time to confront these emotions will enable you to take the first step towards addressing the feedback you have received.

It's not always easy, but with time you will learn how to see these reviews for the little gems they are.

And you'll only lay awake at night sometimes ...

A Mini Task for You

As we saw in this chapter, here are some typical emotions that can be experienced after receiving a bad review:

- anger
- frustration
- irritation
- worry
- nervousness
- rejection
- inadequacy

Dealing with guest feedback is never easy and you will respond emotionally.

This task ensures you have measures in place to recognise these emotional responses so that you can deal positively with the feedback. I guarantee that by removing negative emotions from your decision-making process, you will make better decisions.

Find a review page for a business that is not your own. Find at least five reviews from Detractors and read them and think how that business owner should respond. Now find at least five reviews from Detractors on your own business and take note of the feelings you have while reading them. Which set of reviews generated more of the emotions listed above? See how emotion can cloud your judgement when dealing with bad reviews?

Think about why you felt that way – was it because the guest was right in their feedback? Was it because you knew that changes needed to be made before you received that feedback? Or was it because you felt that the guest was being unfair in their assessment of your business?

Next, write out a plan for dealing with these emotions. You can choose to use the examples I have given or you can create your own – whatever works best for you.

CHAPTER 7

Phase Three – It's Lies, All Lies!

Park needs a pool for people that don't like swimming in the ocean. some people just like to walk on beach not swim. enjoyed our stay very much. staff were very nice and friendly and helpful.

~ Dorothy

Have you put your reviews aside hoping they will just go away? Have you convinced yourself that the negative feedback that guests give you doesn't have any impact on your business?

Are you wondering why you aren't getting bookings through that online travel agent anymore?

Have you tried to respond to the feedback someone left you, only to get stuck halfway, and tell yourself that you'll come back to it?

Have you?

The good news is that you aren't the only one. When someone leaves your business negative feedback online, it's normal to want to ignore it. It's reasonable to think that it will get lost among the other positive reviews that people leave for you.

The bad news?

Every day that negative feedback remains available to people, it *is* doing damage to your business. People *are* judging you on that feedback and they judge harshly if they see you haven't done anything to address or even acknowledge the concerns raised.

The more you ignore reviews and don't respond to them, the more weight that criticism gains. Every day, more and more people use online forums and websites to choose which business they will stay at when on vacation, visit for a meal or go to for an experience.

Understanding the best ways to respond to online feedback and making sure that you get to the bottom of the situations that cause that feedback is one of the most important jobs a business should do today.

Investigating Bad Reviews

The first step you need to take after receiving negative feedback from a guest is to understand why that review was left and determine the circumstances that led to it in the first place. Having a process to investigate the cause of the problem then provides you with two paths to walk down.

The first path is focusing upon the actual issue and dealing with the guest's concerns. The second path is thinking about what your business can update in its processes or offers that will avoid this type of review being given in the future. The good news is that both paths can be travelled simultaneously, so you don't need to worry about a lengthy journey. The following steps will assist you in getting to the root cause of your negative review and help you map out a course of action to deal with it.

Make a Checklist

The best place to start your investigation is with the complaint itself. In my experience, guests will leave feedback about multiple issues.

This is because when guests have one negative experience, all they see are more negatives. If, for example, the complaint is about the cleanliness of your bathrooms, the review will then typically go on to say that the grounds were also unclean, even if they weren't.

The core complaint was about the bathrooms, so this is where you should start. Creating a checklist of each issue raised can help you to break down where your focus needs to be in your investigation and response.

Check the System

The next step you need to take is to find the guest in your booking system. Not all online reviews give you the guest's full details, so there is usually a bit of hunting involved. Once you have found the guest, check whether there are any details on their file that may relate to their feedback. Did they raise an issue with staff? Is there a request for a refund? Was there a call-out to their location while they stayed with you?

If you are unable to find the guest in your booking system, this is when you might need to contact them to ask for more information. At this point I would always offer my contact details for them to reach me directly. This way, the complaint is dealt with offline and I can offer a more personal approach to show that I am considering their complaint seriously.

Ask Your Team

By now you should have a clear idea about who the guest is and what caused the bad experience that generated the review. At this stage, I'd recommend talking to your team about what happened and what was done, if anything, to alleviate the guest's concerns while they were still staying with you. If we look at the earlier example of bathroom cleanliness, checking your cleaning roster and asking the cleaning team if the proper process was followed can give you some understanding if there is merit to the guest's claims. You may find that your processes have fallen down and might need a refresh, or you may need to have a more detailed discussion with the team member responsible for the problem that occurred.

Dealing with Bad Reviews

Once you have investigated the feedback, you can start to formulate a response. There are a few different ways you can respond, whether that be over the phone, via email or on the review site where the feedback was left.

There is no right or wrong method to respond to a bad review. However, if the feedback was left online, remember that future guests can see it, and you don't want to give them the impression that you haven't dealt with the issues that were raised. If you speak with the guest and address their concerns over the phone, make a point of also responding to the online review, mentioning that you've addressed their feedback. For example:

Hi Jane,

Thank you for the feedback about your stay. I am sorry to hear that it was not to the expected standards you have for us, or those that we have for ourselves.

I would like to thank you for allowing me to address your concerns via phone and if you are in the area again we would love to have you stay with us so we can demonstrate that your issue was a one-off.

Safe travels.
Adrian Easdown

Even though you have dealt with the specific complaint directly, anyone else reading your response online will have no idea that happened. If you have learned anything so far is that, there are a lot of people online waiting for you to respond, even if they aren't involved in the situation. That's why there are a few other things you should keep in mind when responding online to customer feedback: never be defensive, never be aggressive, add personality to your response, and don't get personal.

Never Be Defensive

One of the biggest mistakes you can make is being defensive in your responses to customer feedback. Defensiveness shows people that even though you are responding, you haven't taken their feedback on board. Instead, it looks like you are blaming the person for leaving you that review. Even if the guest's review demonstrates their own unreasonable expectations of your business (Remember the weather?), responding with gracious comments like 'Thank you for your feedback' or 'We will take your feedback on board' shows that you care.

Never Be Aggressive

Always remember that a bad review can be turned into a positive guest engagement with someone who is deciding whether or not to stay at your business. Making sure that you don't respond aggressively will show future guests that you are a business that they can interact with positively, even when things don't go right.

For example, an aggressive approach would be:

As I explained to you when you were here, we do NOT offer free wi-fi and nowhere on our website does it say we DO. We are NOT responsible for your incorrect understanding of our services.

This response has capitals in it which can be interpreted as shouting in an online forum. It is also directing blame at the guest by saying 'We are NOT responsible'. It could have been handled more positively with the following approach:

Thanks for your feedback, Kim. We know wi-fi can make a holiday even better and we are sorry that you thought our wi-fi was free. We appreciate the time you have taken to give us your feedback. Safe travels.

The second response, while highlighting that the misunderstanding was on the guest's side, comes off far friendlier. It also shows any potential guests that you don't offer free wi-fi which can avoid the situation recurring in the future.

Add Personality to Your Response

One of the worst things about online responses is that you can't hear voice tone or see body language, and so anyone who reads a response will be impacted by their current mindset.

So, how do you make sure your written response isn't taken the wrong way?

Use your personality.

When we talk, we choose certain words that convey who we are and the type of personality we have; you can use those words in your written responses as well. Adding personality to your response also shows your guests that it is *you* who is responding, not a paid marketing employee or a response from a pre-formulated template.

This is an example of a response to avoid:

Hi. Thank you for your feedback. We have considered the matter and will ensure that this does not occur again.

It's boring, bland and generic. A better response would be:

> *Hi Scott. I have made sure that the offending tree root has been removed – thanks for the heads up! Sorry that you had a hard time putting in your pegs. If you're ever out our way again, give us a shout, we would be glad to have you back.*

The second response brings in the issue that was in the feedback and uses conversational word choices. Reading your responses aloud can help you to hear if they seem robotic.

Don't Get Personal

There will be times when you get a review that's personal. Sometimes the person leaving the review is angry and they take all that anger out on the keyboard and your business. People can leave comments that are unprofessional and specifically target you, or a member of your team. What you must avoid is responding in a similar way. Avoid attacking the reviewer at all costs (even if you really want to respond that way).

We spoke in a previous chapter about dealing with your emotions. Use the exercises in that chapter to help you calm down before responding to a personal attack online.

A response you should avoid is:

> *Hi Guest. We don't need rude guests like you in our park anyway. Your kids caused a riot across the park and you should learn to control them better. We can understand why they behave that way with parents like you.*

Retaliating is always ugly. Instead, you should always take the high road because it then makes the complaint seem out of line while also taking the sting out of it. People will be drawn to the drama of an angry complaint online, so if you respond nicely you will win points with future guests. A better response would be:

Hi Colin. I'm sorry to hear you didn't have a great experience with us. Your kids sure did enjoy the park. They were on their bikes and riding from one end of the park to the other. Our park rule is that helmets should always be worn while riding bikes. We understand if you don't enforce this when you are at home, but the safety of our guests is of prime importance to us. Safe travels.

The second response takes the sting out of the customer complaint and adds a little humour into the mix. However, be careful that you don't come across as too cocky in your response as this may cause more problems for you.

The rule of thumb when dealing with customer feedback is: approach it like you were the person leaving the feedback. If you respond the way you would want to be treated, then you will address your guest's concern while also staying respectful and professional.

A Resource for You

In the previous chapter, we looked at ways that you should and shouldn't respond to guests when dealing with their feedback. To assist you in developing your own responses to guest feedback, you'll find examples on the next page of some of my responses to an assortment of feedback that my businesses have received.

Dear Margo,

I'd like to thank you for the time you have taken to provide us with your valued feedback about your recent stay.

I acknowledge your comments on the following:

'The units were not as clean as they should be. Floors were dirty & dishes needed washing up. I know it's up to the person staying there to do the dishes before they leave but I thought this would be checked.'

My apologies. We do have very high standards when it comes to maintaining cleanliness throughout the park and I am disappointed to hear that we missed these things in your unit.

Thank you for bringing this to our attention. These issues will be dealt with immediately. Feel free to contact me if you have any further comments.

Kind regards,

Adrian

Dear Roger,

I'd like to thank you for the time you have taken to provide us with your valued feedback about your recent stay.

I acknowledge your comments on the following:

'Toilet blocks are a little old and dated.'

'A beautiful place and your willingness to help is outstanding.'

There are plans for a full refurbishment of the park currently out for public consultation. As part of this process the amenities will be replaced. I shall use your feedback as part of this process to help us improve the park.

I am glad you love the park as much as we do. Thank you for scoring us a 10. We do have a wonderful team who put in a lot of effort to maintain the park and we are always happy to help. Feel free to contact me if you have any further comments.

Safe travels!

Adrian

Dear Stephen and Rochelle,

I'd like to thank you for the time you have taken to provide us with your valued feedback about your recent stay.

I acknowledge your comments on the following:

'Not enough park patrol with regards to music noise levels etc.'

'Cleaning once a day first thing in the morning (the toilets were always closed then) when the park is at full capacity isn't enough.'

Inside and outside the school holiday period we do have security guards patrolling the park on Friday and Saturday nights. All other nights Robert and myself conduct regular patrols of the park throughout the night. You would also have been given at check-in the after-hours number, which you were able to call if there was anything worrying you, such as excessive noise that we aren't aware of.

When a park is at a certain capacity the regulations state amenities must be cleaned twice per day. We do this during the entire school holiday period at 4am and again at 2pm. Although the amenities are quite old, we take great pride in keeping them very clean, and I am sorry that you didn't find them to be that way during your stay.

I hope that you enjoyed your stay with us regardless of the above, and we look forward to your return next year.

Please feel free to contact me with any other feedback you may have as your opinion is very important to us.

Thank you,

Adrian

Dear Wendy,

I'd like to thank you for the time you have taken to provide us with your valued feedback about your recent stay.

I acknowledge your comments on the following:

'The amenities are outdated but kept very clean.'

'Our site was quite dirty on our recent stay; it would have been good if some watering had been done to keep the sites at least a little green.'

'I don't really like the key system for access to the amenities and wonder whether the lanyards are washed. A system where a code is entered would be preferable.'

We take great pride in keeping the park very clean and we believe we have a great team helping us achieve this. Thank you for your feedback; we will pass this on to our amenity cleaners.

Due to the lack of rain in Yamba over the past four months, we do have very dry grounds, and we had been advised by council that watering was causing the water usage to be too high, so unfortunately we were unable to water. We have recently raised our concerns with council regarding the dry park grounds and they have allowed us to begin watering again. So along with the rain we have just received, we should have some nice green grass in no time.

The key lanyards are washed and keys and tags are disinfected each fortnight. We recently purchased new lanyards which have now replaced the old ones. A code system for the amenities would be great. There is a refurbishment of the park planned which has recently been approved, and we will use your feedback as part of amenities refurbishment. In the meantime, you are welcome to request no lanyard on your key if you like next time you visit.

Feel free to contact me if you have any further comments.

Kind regards,

Adrian

CHAPTER 8

Phase Four – Whose Fault is It Anyway?

The birds, dropping poop on our car and caravan.
Love seeing the birds and hearing them.

~ Christine

Things go wrong.

Guests have bad experiences.

The best intentions can sometimes result in the worst situations. In a nutshell, sometimes you're going to suck.

Every day, business owners wake up and tell themselves that today is going to be great. Today, they are going to really nail providing gold-star services to their guests.

Unfortunately, that's not how every day goes, and from time to time you may have someone in your team that doesn't deliver, for whatever reason, every time.

And that's okay. We aren't perfect, and we definitely aren't always a bunch of sunshine and rainbows.

The problem is that guests do expect you to deliver a gold-star service for them every time. They don't know that they are the fiftieth guest you checked in that week. They don't know that you didn't get a chance to flag their specific requirements with reception because you were with the plumber all day fixing the blocked showers.

Bad reviews don't always stem from a situation that you can control or manage appropriately and, for the most part, guests will accommodate those mistakes and give you a bit of leeway.

But if you don't have the proper processes in place to manage feedback and possibly avoid these situations in the future, then that leeway will quickly shrink.

Don't Brush Aside The Feedback

Sometimes you'll get feedback from a guest and you'll cringe because it cuts close to the bone. There is no-one who knows your business better than you do, especially the faults. But avoiding these areas of your business can put you in a difficult situation.

As we've seen in previous chapters, guests let their fingers do the walking online long before they come and stay at your business. They may have seen the odd bit of negative feedback listed online, but if the positive reviews far outweigh the negatives then they'll still come to stay. But, the thing is, these guests now have a seed of doubt in their minds, and will be looking out for similar situations.

If they have even a slightly similar experience, they are absolutely going to leave you a bad review online. And when future guests see patterns of negative feedback, this shows that there *is* a real problem at your business that isn't being addressed. This is going to hurt you in the long run as guests simply won't book with your business. Ignoring reviews and not dealing with the feedback that comes with them is one of the worst things you can do.

The Many Pieces of Feedback

There will, of course, be times that things don't go to plan in your business. A guest might have the complete wrong idea about what your business is offering. Someone could have called in sick, so reception was overwhelmed. You might have a team member who has been struggling with performance and has contributed to a poor guest experience. Or someone just forgot to do their task that day. Whatever the case, here are some common pieces of feedback that guests send in and suggestions on how to tackle these problems.

Bad Review Item #54: 'Your toilets weren't clean.'

A common piece of negative feedback is about the cleanliness of shared toilet facilities. Even though you might have a cleaning roster that covers two different intervals a day, having high human traffic visiting these facilities will lead to situations that most people do not want to have to deal with.

Some Dos and Don'ts for This Situation:

- Do have a published cleaning roster for guests to view at the toilet block.
- Do have a cleaning roster for your team to check.
- Do have clear signage in the facilities for guests to contact reception if they find an issue.
- Don't ignore the problem.
- Don't have an ad-hoc cleaning roster.
- Don't avoid team members having clear ownership of cleaning duties.

Bad Review Item #102: 'Your rooms weren't clean.'

Another common trend in negative feedback is related to the cleanliness of rooms. The room could have been dusty when they checked in, or there might have been something left in the bin. There is a big list of reasons that will lead people to think your accommodation is not clean. There will be some items that people won't mind, but that same item could drive another guest to leave you a bad review.

Some Dos and Don'ts for This Situation:

- Do have a procedure for pre-arrival checks on the rooms.
- Do have a documented cleaning process for rooms. By having a uniform approach, you ensure things don't get missed.
- Do have an emergency process in place for when staff are on sick leave to make sure rosters are covered.
- Do make cleaning staff accountable by leaving a 'Cleaned by' card in the room.
- Don't ignore feedback, even if it is a one-off.
- Don't rely on your own concept of what is 'clean'. Ask for input from your team on their views; everyone has their own level of cleanliness.
- Don't assume that things are being done. Have an auditing process and spot checks in place.

Bad Review Item #145: 'There were too many people staying.'

There are going to be times when your business is full to the brim with guests. This kind of occupancy, while great for your bottom line, can lead to negative feedback. People have come to your business to have a nice holiday. Most of the time they haven't bargained for all the other people who are going to be taking a holiday at the same time. Whenever you have high turnover times, like summer holidays, it is best you approach this situation with the mindset that people want to go somewhere quiet, then gently burst that bubble.

Some Dos and Don'ts for This Situation:
- Do manage guests' expectations with email confirmations, and during check-in.
- Do use social media to post photographs demonstrating it is peak season.
- Don't ignore feedback from guests; acknowledge it and give them suggestions on times to use communal facilities.
- Don't ignore your team's wellbeing and ensure they have their allocated breaks.
- Don't assume that everything is running well. Get out and about in order to investigate and monitor processes across your business.

Bad Review Item #234: 'Your facilities need work.'

Running an accommodation business is expensive. There are always some improvements that need to happen. And with so many people using your facilities, *average* wear and tear is not something that impacts you … it's more like *mass* wear and tear. Notes asking you to keep your facilities fresh and modern are some of the most common pieces of feedback that accommodation businesses receive. And I get it: who wouldn't love to renovate their bathrooms every year? The reality is finances are finite, and your business will go through phases when it looks a little tired.

So, how do you manage your budgets and your guest feedback around this issue? I've found that this takes a bit of forward thinking. I look at my revenue and divide up the improvements and maintenance into short-term and long-term needs. Planning up to five years ahead allows me to see how much revenue I need to put aside each year so that I have the cash to make major changes to my park.

Also, by splitting up quick, low-budget items from big-ticket items you can maximise the facilities you do have by making them look fresher. Repainting facilities can be a small investment if you do it yourself. This is a simple solution that will freshen up and extend the life of your facilities. Even if you know that they're long overdue for renovation, making sure that what you do have on offer is as fresh and bright as possible will usually go a long way with guests and lead to moderate reviews rather than bad ones.

Bad Review Item #336: 'Your staff are rude!'

No-one likes confrontation, and aversion to confrontation can sometimes make matters worse. But if you have a pattern of feedback that your team doesn't handle guests appropriately, then this is something you should deal with quickly. A trap that some staff fall into is mimicking the guest's attitude. This is great if the guest presents at reception full of beans and happy, but if the guest is snarky, you don't want your staff to send that same attitude back. Walk a mile in your client's shoes. One thing I like to remind my staff is that they don't know what the guest has been through before they arrive in front of you. Knowing how the situation came about and then working through the problem can ensure you are supporting your team appropriately while giving the guest the outcome they expect.

Walk a Mile in Your Client's Shoes

I once had a couple who entered reception and they were chalk and cheese in their attitudes. The lady was pleasant, seemed easy to please and was smiling the whole time. Her husband was the complete opposite – he was grumpy, aggressive towards the staff and looked like he was sucking a prune. The staff dealt with the couple professionally, but I was curious as to how a couple could be complete polar opposites. I made an effort to visit the couple later that day and, coincidentally, when I visited, the husband was out. I had a great chat to the lady. It turned out she had terminal cancer. She had been able to deal with the emotion and was at a point of accepting her illness, but unfortunately her husband was not at that stage yet. He was angry with the world and it showed. Armed with this information, it was easier to empathise with their situation. It is key for anyone working in customer service to never assume anything and walk a mile in their client's shoes.

The Guest Was Misinformed

Let's take the example that one of your team members has had a bad review written about them, but you've discovered it was the result of the guest's unreasonable expectations. Your team member had provided the guest with your business's policies in a way that was respectful and tempered. But on not getting their way, the guest may leave a bad review. In this scenario, an appropriate response to the guest would be:

Dear Mary

Thank you for taking the time to review our business. We are sorry you did not have a good experience with us. As our friendly team member shared with you while you were here, we don't allow dogs in the park, which is stated on our website and was also in your confirmation email. We also have a very helpful sign at reception on check-in.

Adrian

By responding in a friendly way with factual information that was originally provided to the reviewer, you highlight that the review is not accurate and that the guest was in the wrong. You don't need to take on all the reviewer's points they might have left about your team member, but with a small note about how friendly your staff member is, you can counter the negative feedback.

The Guest Was Aggressive

A bad review can result from a situation that spiralled out control. For example, a guest may have interacted with your staff aggressively for whatever reason, and your team member may have been aggressive and rude in their response. Once you have got to the bottom of the situation that occurred, the best response to have with that guest is as follows:

Dear David

Thank you for contacting us, your feedback is important. Please contact our office on (##) #### #### so that I can discuss this with you personally.

Adrian

If there has been a situation with high emotion, no matter who was at fault, the best way to deal with it is to discuss it with the guest directly. Continuing the fight online will only make matters worse as potential guests will view this back and forth. There is never a situation that warrants a guest behaving aggressively towards your staff, so making sure that your staff knows they can walk away from those situations is always the best course of action. I have an established policy in my business that staff must refer angry guests directly to management so they don't need to deal with them.

Making sure that you address all situations in your business as they come up is a fantastic way to avoid bad reviews. But if that situation has already occurred, then learning how to use bad reviews to improve your business to avoid more will ensure that you are constantly moving forward.

A Mini Task for You

The task that sits in front of you now is the best way to approach the feedback that has been given to you. Start with a report from the system that you use to record guest feedback. The date range you enter into the system for your report will be determined by your target date range to respond to previous reviews (for example, the past three months). The best kind of report to use is a spreadsheet so that you can add more columns.

On your spreadsheet, add columns for the following: online feedback, star, other feedback, cause, response, outcome and process changes.

Start with one review site or social media account and match up the feedback that has been received with the guest output from the booking system. Enter this information into the column 'online feedback'. If you or your staff received feedback verbally, via email or through a survey response, capture this in the column 'other feedback'.

At this stage, it's important to work out exactly what steps need to be taken to address the feedback and what you did to resolve the issue. These historical records can come in handy if the same guest provides more bad reviews in the future.

When it comes to customer service issues, including in your spreadsheet the steps that you took with individual team members can also help you with staff development and one-on-one discussions. This will be discussed in later chapters.

What you will be left with after completing each column, is a spreadsheet containing feedback, the root causes, issues and what steps you need to take to address the feedback and prevent the situation from reoccurring.

The more information you add, the more detailed your record of events will be.

You should now be able to see patterns forming in your guest feedback that highlight key areas that most need to be improved.

The next step is to formulate your responses to guests. As seen in previous chapters, it is important to include the key points from the guest's feedback and then provide the steps taken to correct these.

This task should be completed on a weekly basis to ensure you are on top of feedback received from various channels. If you are unable to do this yourself each week, train a team member and make it a part of their weekly duties.

CHAPTER 9

Phase Five – Round Up the Troops, It's Time to Deal

All of the staff we dealt with were very accommo-dating, we needed to hire an extra set of linen – but that was sorted for us straight away.

- Lisa

B ad reviews are bad, right? I mean it says it right there: bad. B-A-D.

Here's the definition of 'bad' from the Oxford Dictionary:

bad, *adjective*

1. Of poor quality or a low standard,
    bad eyesight.
    Synonyms: substandard, poor, inferior, second-rate, second-class, unsatisfactory, inadequate, unacceptable, not up to scratch, not up to par, deficient, imperfect, defective, faulty, shoddy, amateurish, careless, negligent

    ...

2.   Not such as to be hoped for or desired; unpleasant or unwelcome,
bad news.
Synonyms: unpleasant, disagreeable, unwelcome, unfortunate, unfavourable, unlucky, adverse, nasty

...

But what if I told you that the best thing that could ever happen to your business is a bad review?

No, I'm not mad. And, no, this isn't one of those reverse-psychology situations where everything that is bad is good, and vice versa.

A bad review is a piece of gold that is hand delivered to you.

People pay experts thousands of dollars every year to tell them what is wrong with their business. But all you need to do is go online and you can get that information for free.

People are taking time out of their daily lives and literally telling you all the things you need to do to improve your business.

That's why a bad review is a good thing. No, scratch that – a phenomenal thing.

Every bad review has the potential to show how amazing you are at customer service. It can help you prioritise improvements to your park, hotel or restaurant. It can also win you guests that might not have considered staying at your business until they read your responses to feedback that was left for you.

But you need to have a plan to deal with bad reviews to maximise their potential. In the work I do with clients, I have developed a framework to help them find ways to improve their businesses and open up their profits to double-digit growth. I call this my R.E.V.I.E.W. process. The best thing about this framework is I can adapt it to multiple situations and problems, it is an effective method of high-lighting areas that require improvement and then implementing change in these areas. This chapter shows how to use my proven framework, the R.E.V.I.E.W. process, to deal with bad reviews.

The R.E.V.I.E.W. Process

Over the years, I have developed and used an easy and effective process to get the most out of the reviews that guests give me. I have rolled this process out over the multiple businesses that I manage, and my clients' businesses, and I have yet to find fault with approaching feedback from guests in this way.

R: Rate the Feedback

The first thing that I do when I receive less-than-desirable feedback is rate it against the ratings systems I have in my business. We talked in Chapter 4 about the Net Promoter Score (NPS) and the 5-star system. These are the metrics that I use to rate guest feedback. Once I understand where this particular feedback sits, I then choose the most appropriate method for dealing with the feedback.

I also rate feedback against my own expectations for guests when they come and stay with us. Our business plan details these expectations in a simple checklist, and allows me to formulate a solid response to the guest. It also shows me where the business is failing and where I need to spend time improving the business.

E: Examine the Feedback

After I have rated the feedback, I then spend time examining it and considering the situations that created the bad review in the first place. This involves asking the team what happened and if the guest left any other feedback at check-out or throughout their stay. I check staff and cleaning rosters for the relevant days, as well as our databases to get as much detail about the guest as possible.

I also take the time to take a walk in the guest's shoes. I will look at the place they stayed, whether that be a cabin or a campsite.

Once I have managed to piece together the feedback from the guest's perspective, I add this to the rating form so that we have all the information – from the business's side and the guest's side – that led to that bad review.

It is also important to evaluate what category the feedback belongs to. Sample categories that I use are:

- Staff/Customer Service
- Infrastructure/Capital Works
- Grounds/Amenities
- Cabins/Rooms
- Cleanliness/Cleaning.

By categorising your feedback, you can prioritise responses and also budget for improvements. Remember when we were talking about *Bad Review Item #234: 'Your facilities need work'*? We talked about managing budgets and allocating expenditure. If you collate your feedback into categories, you can make informed decisions about where spending your hard-earned dollars will be of the most impact to your guests, rather than just going on gut feel. You can also better identify where staff need more training or supervision, or where your processes need some polishing.

V: Visualise the Feedback

Seeing your business from the reviewer's point of view is key to understanding why you received the feedback you did, and it can usually give you a good indication of how you are going to deal with that guest. The more you understand the feedback, the better placed you will be to respond to it and improve your business for future guests. It can also help you to decide whether to throw the feedback into the bucket of misunderstandings, and focus on turning that review into an opportunity for great customer service instead.

Let's take the example of a guest expecting free wi-fi. You might not offer free wi-fi, and there is nothing that says you should. But you receive feedback from a guest that centres around the fact you don't offer it. For the life of you, you can't understand why the guest made this assumption about your business. Having investigated the situation and gathered the data about your guest, you see that they were an international traveller, travelling around Australia, and they were in Sydney until moving to your business along the coast.

What you now have is a bit of information that shows why you received the complaint. Most accommodation businesses in Europe have free wi-fi; it's so common in Europe that you can pick up the free wi-fi of restaurants, cafes and hotels while walking in the street. Plus the guest has just left a big tourist location in Sydney that has free wi-fi, so they are probably operating under the assumption that everywhere in Australia has free wi-fi – just like Europe. Even though you don't list anything about free wi-fi on your website or in any documentation sent to the guest, chances are they have added their own assumptions onto your business when deciding to stay with you. Visualising the feedback from the guest's point of view enables you to understand the review.

I: Implement Changes Based on Feedback

Once I have the whole situation mapped out from the guest's perspective, I take two major steps: the first step is formulating a response to the guest and the second is trying to avoid the same situation happening again. This stage can be easy to address if you're dealing with a straightforward matter like an unclean bathroom, which would lead to an update to the cleaning rosters. But it can also be a difficult stage to address too.

One of the difficulties of constantly dealing with many different people is that you won't be able to accommodate everybody's tastes all the time. And the reality is you shouldn't be trying to do this anyway. But that doesn't mean that one-off feedback or feedback stemming from a misunderstanding should be ignored.

If we go back to the wi-fi example, this feedback was the result of the guest's incorrect assumption. You might have listed on your website that wi-fi is an additional cost, so it would be easy to brush off the feedback and not do anything about it. But you can still address this feedback for future guests by including a mention of the cost for wi-fi in booking confirmations. You could also move the information about your wi-fi to a different section of your website, making it even more visible that you don't offer it for free.

Don't be scared to explain in your review responses that you have made changes due to their feedback. There is nothing wrong with eating a bit of humble pie; the point of implementing change based on feedback is to improve your business and processes, but also to demonstrate to those who read your reviews and responses that you are open to feedback. Taking the time to include this in your responses can also turn a guest into an advocate for your business.

Even if it means only slightly tweaking what you're already doing, it's always worthwhile implementing changes based on feedback.

E: Evaluate the Impact of the Changes

You will generally need to wait a long time for a guest to return to your business to gauge the impact of the changes you implement based on their feedback. Some guests might not ever return. To evaluate if the changes you make reduce negative feedback around that issue, you need to be both patient and proactive at the same time. Sound a little contradictory? Let me go into a bit more detail.

Being Patient

The easiest way to evaluate the effectiveness of changes to your business is to gauge whether negative feedback reduces or increases. If negative feedback about that issue stops, then you can be comfortable thinking that the changes you made addressed the issue.

But what if I told you there was a better, more proactive way to see if the changes you made addressed the issue?

The best way to collate feedback from your guests is via an After-departure Survey. Use your booking system or online software such as SurveyMonkey and, on the afternoon after they depart, send them a survey. There are a number of benefits to providing an After-departure Survey rather than simply waiting for online reviews. You will typically receive more feedback, but you will also reduce the number of bad online (and publically available) reviews by giving your guests an opportunity to give you feedback internally.

Being Proactive

If, for example, the bulk of your negative feedback is about the cleanliness of your business, you can make proactive changes by updating your cleaning rosters and by implementing a uniform process for cleaning particularly troublesome areas. Also, encourage your reception staff to ask guests about their experience as they check out. Better still, introduce a feedback process called a Mid-stay Survey allowing you to obtain feedback from your guests while they are still staying with you. By engaging with the guests directly during their stay, you can gauge quickly if the changes you made are working or if you need to make more tweaks to avoid more negative feedback being left for you.

Continuous Evaluation

Another fantastic way to ensure that you are making the most of your bad reviews is to evaluate and check past feedback against the feedback that is being left for you today. If you see that negative feedback has reduced or has stopped, then chances are you have a pretty good business on your hands. If there are other patterns of negative feedback appearing, you may have another area of your business that needs to be looked at. Using past critical feedback as a guide for current processes also allows you to see the issues that your guests focus on and can steer you away from problems before they occur.

W: Winning Business

Once you have been through the first five steps of the R.E.V.I.E.W. process, you will be in a situation to win more business. The more you show your guests – past, present and future – that you care about their feedback and make changes to your business because of their feedback, the more business you will win.

As we have seen in previous chapters, some people leave critical reviews because they want you to make changes to ensure that future guests don't have the same bad experience they did. Your guests want you to deliver on the commitments you make as a business; they want you to succeed.

A business that does not act on guest feedback is the worst kind of business you can run: one that ignores the possibility for greatness. We are all on a journey of continual improvement, it is just that some of us take it more seriously than others.

A Resource for You

Now that we have explored the ways that you can deal with guest feedback, and you have a robust tracking document, we've reached the final step – responding to the feedback online. These additional examples will help to reinforce what we have learnt so far.

As mentioned in previous chapters, there are good and bad ways to respond to guests. The best review responses take something that was mentioned in the review and use it in the response. When approaching bad reviews, bring your tracking sheet into play. You can weave the information you've discovered into your responses in a friendly and positive way.

Over the page are some more real review examples that my businesses have received, along with the responses I gave. I start with positive review examples and then provide some bad ones too. These examples should give you a good starting point for your own responses. Over time, you'll find that you will be able to write responses quickly and easily without any hesitation. You'll also develop a number of personalised templates that will make it easier for you to deal efficiently with feedback left for your business. Of course, if you combine the following examples and the ones from previous chapters you will have a decent number to be used in your own business.

Positive Reviews

Review

Hi Team

Had a wonderful stay with you. Loved the bikes you had available for us to rent. The kids haven't stopped talking about them since we left. (Thanks for that, now I know what's on the Christmas list this year.)

See you next year.

Happy Guest

89

Response

Hi Happy Guest

It was a pleasure having you stay with us on your holiday, and thank you for your great review. We can send you the name of our bike supplier, if you like? We're glad you had a good time and can't wait for you to return again soon.

> *Safe travels*
> *Adrian*

Review

Hi Guys

We stayed for a week, loved it and have booked for next year for two months. However we hope the price doesn't go up too much, as not only us, but a lot of other annuals won't be able to afford to go there. Clean amenities, lovely staff and great bowling greens.

> *See you next year!*
> *Janet*

Response

Hi Janet

It was a pleasure having you stay with us on your holiday, and thank you for your great review.

We can't wait to see you again next year and will do our best to provide you and all your friends with great value for money on your next stay with us.

We're glad you had a good time and can't wait to see you next year.

> *Safe travels*
> *Adrian*

Review

Hi Team

Great location and awesome little town. Park the car and walk everywhere. Have been coming here every year since I was born. Highly recommend.

See you next year!

Tracey

Response

Hi Tracey

It was a pleasure having you stay with us on your holiday, and thank you for your great review. We always know it's summer when we see you coming through the gates with your kids. We're so happy you keep coming back. We're glad you had a good time and can't wait for you to return soon.

Safe travels

Adrian

Bad Reviews

Review

Management was quite rude to my family on our last stay there and this Easter we will not be staying there as our booking was cancelled without notice. So if you do book here be very careful with your booking as they may give away without notice. Best bet would be to stay somewhere with lower fees and better accommodation and facilities and better management.

Angry Guest

Response

Hi Angry Guest

I'm sorry that your experience with us was not a positive one.

Thanks for spending the time with me on the phone to talk about your situation. We have spoken to our booking agent and they advised us that the payment for your booking was unsuccessful.

Our reception team did their best in sorting that out for you when you checked-in – we know these things sometimes happen.
We hope the rest of your stay was a pleasant one and glad it was sorted out in the end.
Safe travels
Adrian

Review

Very limited concrete sites for 21-foot van. No double slabs. Disappointing that you had to stay in a particular area with a dog. Grass site we had was uneven and sandy. The exit was difficult to manoeuvre with a large van.
Heather

Response

Hi Heather
I'm sorry that your experience with us was not a positive one.
Thank you for your feedback about the double slabs. You'll be happy to hear that we have started construction on some for the park. This was made possible because of suggestions from guests like you.
As it was Christmas we had you in our overflow area. This wasn't due to the dog, but because the other areas of our park were full, which is unavoidable during peak holiday season.
I'm sure if you came back again in a month or two you would be able to enjoy the other areas of our park.

Have a great drive to Queensland.
Safe travels
Adrian

Review

They insult you after they take your money. Do yourself a favour, don't stop there. Go somewhere else. Management doesn't deserve their position here.

Naomi

Response

Hi Naomi

I'm sorry that your experience with us was not a positive one.

I tried to contact you via the phone number we had in our records and have left you a message. I would be more than happy to discuss your concerns and see if I can work with you on them. Our number is (##) #### ####.

I look forward to hearing from you soon.

Adrian

PART THREE

'HOW TO AVOID BAD REVIEWS'

CHAPTER 10

Social Media is Your Friend

One male cleaner was very informative on the local fishing, but he forgot to tell the fish!!

- Paul

Social media is the enemy, right?

If it wasn't for the invention of page after page on the internet giving your business negative reviews, then the whole problem would just go away.

The reality is, people were talking badly about your business, and every business on the planet, long before the invention of the internet and social media. The only thing the internet did was create a space where this information could be shared with the whole world.

Social media is just word-of-mouth on steroids and in full Hulk form. The information and details being shared are the same; the format is all that's changed.

And just like word-of-mouth, there are ways that you can intercept and alter the course of people's opinions long before they even think about coming to your business.

When I work with my clients on improving their use of social media in their business, I tell them to take a proactive approach, and make a point of showing them how being active and informative online with their past guests is a great way to turn negative reviews into positive ones.

I have also shown clients how they can use social media to set the stage for future guests and avoid bad reviews from hitting their profiles. All you need to do is embrace social media and make it a key component of your marketing and business models.

If you can't beat them, join them. Let me show you how I have helped several businesses improve their online engagement and build a foundation for double-digit growth.

Find the Best Social Media and Review Sites for Your Business

There is a huge amount of social media options, along with some topnotch review sites, available for people to access. Literally hundreds. So how do you figure out the best ones for your business – the ones that will put you in touch with your guests? To help cut through the multitude of options, I have created a top-five list of must-have social media accounts for businesses operating in the accommodation and tourism industries: Facebook, Instagram and Twitter. You should also ensure that you have an account for the top review sites in the accommodation industry: TripAdvisor and Booking.com.

Facebook

With some two billion users, the number-one social media platform is Facebook, so you should absolutely include it in your marketing plan. You will get the most engagement with guests on this platform because it allows you – and everyone else with a Facebook account – to interact with each other easily. Facebook also has several paid advertising options. These allow you to target guests across the platform and can put your business in front of people who are searching for accommodation in your area. Facebook stores a *lot* of information on its users and can target advertising to specific terms, just like Google. If you are not yet on Facebook, put this book down and go set up your business's Facebook profile. It is easy to do and should not be put off any longer.

Instagram

The massively successful photo-sharing platform, Instagram, is another form of social media I highly recommend for your business. This platform allows you to generate interest for your business with pictures rather than words. By sharing photos and videos that highlight your accommodation facilities and the surrounding area, you connect with an audience who will see what your business can offer on their next holiday. Instagram is more popular with the younger generations; however, more and more, members of older generations are jumping on the platform. If your target demographic is families, then Instagram will assist you in winning over the younger family members who will recommend your business to their parents if they see you are active on the platform. Photos that work well for accommodation businesses on Instagram include sunsets, sunrises and landscapes. Put plenty of these on your profile, along with shots of your business, and your followers will grow rapidly.

Twitter

Some people are quick to discount Twitter; however, I've found that it is a very worthwhile platform to be on from a business perspective. Users of Twitter are a very dedicated group, and interact in a way that does not happen on other social media platforms. Businesses that interact with their guests on Twitter, especially when it comes to complaint handling, can further their reach by winning fans who have thousands of followers. Twitter is also a great platform to get the word out about your business, interact with other local businesses and highlight your local area. It may not be one for you in the end; however, it is well worth checking out to see how you could incorporate it into your social media plan.

TripAdvisor

If you are in the accommodation or tourism industries and you aren't using TripAdvisor, you are doing something wrong. TripAdvisor is the number-one site for reviews about the accommodation and tourism industries. It is basically free advertising. Being active and engaged on this site showcases your business, and shows that you are in control of your profile which, in turn, helps you engage with guests (both past and future). You can highlight specific elements about your business on the site while showing off your business's location. The best part about this social media platform – particularly in comparison to Facebook, Instagram and Twitter – is that the users are specifically looking for an accommodation experience that your business offers. They are generally already engaged and ready to start making decisions on which businesses to use. The better your business looks on this site, the better your business will do. And the best part: there are booking forms on this platform that allows guests to book with you right away.

Booking.com

Booking.com offers similar options and features to TripAdvisor, and provides guests the option to look both at reviews on businesses and make their decisions. The reason it pays to be on both of these sites instead of just one is simply a matter of numbers and preferences. The reason there are so many successful sites that offer the same thing is because users often simply prefer one over the other. While managing multiple profiles across similar social platforms may seem like a drag, being active across the top two will ensure you target the highest number of potential guests.

Find More Social Media Platforms

While my top-five list of platforms will get you off to a great start in connecting your business to guests, there is a simple way to find more worthwhile platforms to incorporate into your marketing and business models.

The place to start is Google – the search engine that is used by more people every second of every day than any other. Because it's the number-one search engine, chances are your guests will head here first to find places they want to visit and stay when coming to your business's location. So do what they would and perform a Google search on your business's city, town or area, and look at the first page of the results. You will find that the first lot of results are ads. Seventy per cent of Google users don't look at the ads; this is referred to as 'ad blindness'.[4] The assumption is that people don't trust the paid result. Instead, it is the organic results – the results after the ads delivered via the Google algorithms – that people trust, even if they have to work harder to reach them.

So, one by one, look through the results to see if your business is listed and if there are reviews or interactions by guests about your business. If you find one platform has more mentions of your business than another then, you might want to consider swapping them around or also including it in your digital strategy. There is no limit to how many profiles you create and manage; however, be aware that the more platforms you are on, the more work these profiles will be to maintain.

Decide Where to Prioritise Your Efforts

There are a few ways that you organise your approach to win you great business without sucking up too much of your time. If your booking system is like mine, you can see which sites your booking traffic is coming from. If you notice that one online platform brings in more bookings than another, you can spend more time on that site than the others. But don't ignore the other platforms, as lower booking traffic can also be a good indicator of bad reviews. Traffic to your booking system may be down on one platform over another due to some negative reviews being left there. That's why it's important that you regularly check your chosen platforms and respond to reviews.

Include Your Team

Opening your social media profiles for your team to maintain is a fantastic way to reduce the amount of time you personally spend managing multiple profiles. The benefit of having a team to maintain the profiles means that you can also bring a fresh perspective to what you post. Whether young or old, all of us have a different approach to what we want to see and interact with on any given day. Posting a variety of different items can make your profiles stand out from others.

SOCIAL MEDIA IS YOUR FRIEND

Go High Tech

There are many intelligence systems and social media management platforms that you can purchase, for a relatively low cost, that will allow you to both manage reviews left for your business and maintain your social media profiles. Intelligence programs like ReviewPro and Revinate notify you when someone has written a review on your business so that you don't have to check each individual profile across multiple sites. Similarly, management platforms such as Hootsuite and Buffer allow you to preset your posts across multiple social media platforms and monitor engagement with users on your profiles, and manage them all from one location.[5]

One of the best features of these intelligence systems and management platforms is the ability to set up surveillance streams that notify you when someone mentions your business or the location of your business online, but doesn't interact with your profile. For example, it is possible with Hootsuite and Buffer to be notified that a user on Twitter commented on your business's general location looking for accommodation suggestions. You can then respond, providing the name of your business. You will have then connected with a potential customer without manually having to search through Twitter yourself. Adopting technology like this will allow you to engage with the public in ways that you might not have even thought about before.

Have a Plan

One of the biggest mistakes that business owners make when getting on social media is not having a clear plan about what they will say on that platform. They jump onto a platform and start posting random things about their business or the area they are located, or they use every interaction as a sales tool for their business. These approaches don't work. The one thing that you should keep in mind when interacting on social media is that each platform is, first and foremost, a place where people come to connect.

Imagine that you are at a party and there are two people talking to you. One of them is sharing a funny story about something that happened to them and the other is talking only about their job. Which person are you likely to want to continue a conversation with? The first one, right? This is the same on social media. Users do not want to be constantly sold things. The occasional offer or reminder that you are a business is completely fine, but mixing up your sales message with other non-sales related items will help you grow your fan base and encourage people to interact with you. There is a rule that gives a guide for businesses posting on social media. The 60/30/10 rule – which is a guide for businesses posting on social media – states that 60% of your posts should be engaging content, 30% should be shared content from others, and 10% should be sales related.

Having a plan is important; you need to spend time looking ahead to decide what information your guests will find interesting and relevant. If, for example, you offer accommodation in a beach-side town, sharing information on Facebook about sunscreen, and daily high- and low-tides will give people another reason to come to your page.

The more information that you share on your social media that is relevant to your guests' lives, the more likely they are to come and hang out with you online.

A Mini Task for You

For this chapter's task, you are going to create a social media strategy that will win guests' hearts and put you ahead of your competition. To do this, you need to establish social media goals, standards and values.

Social Media Goals

I recommend using the S.M.A.R.T. goal-setting method to build your strategy. This will allow you to establish goals that are, according to the acronym, Specific, Measurable, Attainable, Relevant and Time-bound.

The S.M.A.R.T. acronym was first coined in the 1980s by George T Doran and is now one of the most well-circulated social media strategies.

First, be **Specific** and determine who your audience is, what their interests are, whether your business can fulfil their interests, and why they would want to do business with your brand.

Second, choose a specific goal that can be **Measured,** such as a percentage increase of sales, revenue or engagement.

Third, choose a percentage increase that is realistic and **Attainable.** Ask yourself if the organisation has the resources to reach your goal and, if not, determine what it will take to get there. It's better to scale back and create accurate projections rather than choose exaggerated metrics you can't reach.

Fourth, make sure your chosen goal makes sense and is **Relevant** for your business; it should support both the brand vision and core values.

Finally, create a **Timeline** that can realistically be achieved. If necessary, break up large chunks of your goal into smaller monthly, weekly and daily tasks.

Social Media Standards

Now that you have your goals for your social media strategy, the next step is to determine some best practices for your online content. Images, videos, copy and all other types of content that you post should be optimised for a wider reach and to reflect the quality of your business.

Your audience pays attention to the little details and you should too, so share content on a regular basis that speaks to your brand values.

You need to engage with followers on social media every day and post high-quality content on a consistent basis to build an audience of brand advocates.

I recommend the following social media standards:

- **Image quality:** don't post images that are blurry, pixelated, low-quality or contain off-brand messaging. A poorly sized cover photo or slightly pixelated profile image can result in negative brand association and loss of audience.

- **Video quality:** all videos should be high-resolution and present information that your audience will appreciate and enjoy.

- **Copy quality:** if you advertise your brand as being professional, your shared content needs to sound professional. Pay attention to your spelling, grammar and punctuation to ensure your posts are error free.

- **Posting frequency:** make sure you're not posting too much or too little: too much and you become annoying, too little and people forget who you are. There's a balance that needs to be found.

Remember that you only have one chance to make a great first impression, so the quality of your posts and visual elements need to be perfect.

Social Media Value

The next thing you need to establish is what kind of value you offer your guests on social media and how you are going to interact with them. I'm not talking about providing discount offers if they 'like' or 'follow' you; you need to provide something to your guests that will help them in their lives. For example, you might provide weather updates, pass on information about local traffic situations when you know your guests are travelling into your area. You can also provide tips on best camping practices or provide highlights of the local area that guests might want to see when staying with you.

Whatever you choose to do, the best rule of thumb is to ask yourself the question: 'Will this post help someone who follows me?' If you answer yes, then your social media accounts are likely to increase in popularity.

Branding

One of the most important things to do when setting up your social media profiles and planning your approach is to ensure that you have a consistent brand across the channels you've chosen. Ensuring that you have the same profile picture on your Facebook, Twitter and Instagram accounts lets followers identify you easily on different platforms. The company logo works incredibly well for this purpose. When adding images and video to your social media channels, cross-posting them on all of your accounts is another way to create a cohesive brand. While there will be some followers who are connected to your business on multiple channels, most of your followers will be a separate audience, so duplication is okay. Taking the time to add watermarks or business logos to your images is another great way to brand your social media content and profiles.

Additional Considerations

- Customise posting frequency by using social media intelligence and management platforms.

- Create content that speaks to all of your audiences, not just one stream. For example, include content for younger and older generations.

- Add variety to your social media posts.

- Include timely and topical posts speaking to current events that relate to your business.

- Interact with other social media accounts that are in the same industry as your business, especially those that are local to your own. And take the time to interact with your followers' accounts and guests who've stayed with you.

If you use these social media best practices to build your social media strategy, you'll be well on your way towards achieving your business goals.

CHAPTER 11

Customers Are People Too

Very pleasant. The only noise was those bloody plovers
but I guess that is just nature.

~ Brian

Working with people can be difficult sometimes.
Everybody is different and there are times when you just don't get along with some people.

And that is completely fine.

There are also times when you make mistakes. That's okay too because you are a human being and you're not perfect.

And there are times when your guests make mistakes; they might assume something instead of asking. And you know what? That's perfectly okay too.

What I am getting at is that there are always going to be situations when people are in the mix.

The core foundation of the process I have developed working within my own and others' businesses is always remember that guests are people too. They make mistakes, they can be angry, they can be disappointed, they can be happy, they can be sad, and occasionally they can be wrong.

What you need to do from a business perspective is to make sure that even if you are not the cause of whatever situation a guest might be dealing with, you don't make it worse. You also need to show to your guests that you are a person too.

By showing your humanity, warts and all, you build trust with your guests. And the best tool a business owner can have up their sleeve is trust.

Why?

Because trust removes doubt. It gives you wiggle room when things go wrong. And, most importantly, it can help you to avoid bad reviews and drive your business through unprecedented growth year on year. This chapter gives you an insight into some of the successful methods my clients have used while implementing my R.E.V.I.E.W. process.

It's a Relationship, Not a Transaction

Every relationship is built on the foundation of trust. From relationships with friends and family members, through to relationships with movie stars and politicians. These relationships all hinge on one five-letter word: TRUST. You may not think of it that way, but trust is fundamentally the basis of every interaction you have with guests. You are providing experiences within a relationship, not a transaction or an exchange of goods and services.

A relationship is simply several interactions between you and another human being. A long and lasting relationship is a group of interactions spread over time, and the strength of that relationship is judged by the amount of trust that has been built over that time. While this is a very simplified explanation of what people think of as a relationship, it is important to see it this way. Make no mistake – you are in a relationship with each of your guests.

If you consider your guests and their experiences with you and your business as a relationship, you will be able to break down all your interactions, no matter how big or small, and see the elements of trust you have built. Once you look at your business this way, you will know where you can deliver services that target guests at their heart rather than their pocket – and trust me, your business will thrive.

How to Build Trust

People won't stay at your business if they don't trust you, and these days review sites provide the ultimate display of the trust that others have placed in you and your business. If you take control of building trust with your guests while they stay with you, their online reviews will demonstrate with ease to future guests that you are trustworthy and that your business is the right choice for their holidays and experiences.

There are a lot of ways you can build trust with guests, so I will break down a few of these. You don't have to implement them all; choose a few or try out different ones to see which ones work for you and your business.

Just Be Yourself

This seems simple enough; however, I can guarantee there have been times when you've interacted with a guest and you haven't truly been yourself. And you know what? They can tell. For example, think back to a time when you've presented a complaint to a business you interacted with and the person was cold or robotic with you. More than likely this lead you to feel like they weren't listening to you, which probably made you feel frustrated, if not angry. Even if they were listening to you, you felt like they weren't.

How did you treat them? Let's be honest, if we were the guest in that situation, and it wasn't resolved, the next place we would go is somewhere we could be heard – somewhere like the INTERNET.

The more you are yourself and you talk to your guests exactly like you would a friend or family member, the more you will build trust that you are listening to their concerns. Even if they don't walk away with a discount, they will still feel that they got their message across.

I have done some things for my businesses over the years, that I now laugh at. There are also things that I am really proud of. There is a yearly event I jump into that I both loathe and love at the same time, that really shows how I throw myself into my businesses: playing Santa. I love it because there really is nothing better than seeing a kid handed a present by the big man in red; the way their faces light up warms your heart like nothing else. Then there is the polyester suit, the typical scorching hot Aussie summer and the sweat … lots and lots of sweat. You do what you have to do to make sure your guests have a great time, though!

Treat Guests Like Individuals

The best way to build trust with your guests is to spend a little time getting to know who they are. This doesn't need to be anything bigger than knowing their names. At my business, we can see the guests arrive in their vehicles, so we print out the arrivals that are due and take note of the guest's car registration. That way, the moment our guest comes into reception we can welcome them with their name. You would be amazed at the way our guests react when this happens; they feel special and like we already know them. This initial interaction immediately builds a more personal relationship. It means we are already a long way into establishing trust with the guest, which is a valuable head start should anything negative happen during their stay.

Be Curious About Your Guests

It would be fantastic if you could spend large chunks of your day getting to know your guests, but the reality is that you're running a business and every moment is precious. That doesn't mean you can't find small moments to ask questions and find out more about your guests. We have a standing policy in all our parks for the staff to be as personable and curious about our guests as possible. It isn't something that we enforce – not everyone is comfortable asking people they don't know questions. But taking the time to ask pet names, kids' names and taking note of little bits of information that your guests share, can quickly build trust with a guest because it shows them that you're interested and keen to interact.

Making sure that you pay attention to your guests when they interact with you is important; you can discover a lot about them, and you can also step in to help them when things go bad.

I remember a time when we had an older guest come into the reception area to ask us if we had a payphone and how much it was to call emergency services on 000. My reception staff thought it was an odd question, so they told him that he didn't need to pay to call 000; they also told him that he could make that call for free from his mobile.

He listened to what they had to say and then went on a tangent about not being sure how much calls were from his mobile and if he had enough credit to call 000 or not. My team became concerned about this guest and queried him further and he divulged that there was something wrong with his wife. One of my team members went with the guest and found his wife was having a stroke. My team were able to provide first aid to the guest and arrange for the emergency services to come and attend to the guest's wife.

People deal with crisis situations differently, and I often wonder what would have happened if my team had just brushed off the guest's odd behaviour and not queried him further. As I said, it pays to ask questions and pay attention to your guests in all scenarios.

Don't Be a Flake

There are going to be times when your business doesn't meet guest expectations. For example, a guest may find your shower facilities aren't as clean as they believe they should be. If guests raise concerns like this, then you need to deal with the concerns. There will always be different ways that you can handle complaints in your business, but your typical response should include a clear timeframe for when the problem will be addressed. And you must meet that timeframe! If you don't deliver, guests will think that you are untrustworthy and your business will be in danger of receiving negative feedback. Most guests will give you leeway the first time they raise an issue with you, but they will not be as forgiving the second or third time.

Ask for Feedback

I've found that building trust is an interesting process: the more I seek feedback, the more trust I receive. Providing more opportunities for guests to engage with me also opens up more opportunities to deal with potential situations that may lead to negative feedback.

Even if you only ask one question like, 'How has your stay been?', asking for feedback demonstrates that you are open to learning from guests because it provides an opportunity for them to ask questions or raise concerns with you that you can then address.

Communication Is the Key

Miscommunication is one of the biggest drivers behind people leaving bad reviews for a business. The clearer you are in your communications with a guest, the more likely it is that your business will avoid criticism. Even if you have emailed guests their check-in confirmation including crucial details, chances are that, upon arrival, most guests will not have read this. By reiterating this information as they check in and clearly communicating expectations of them during their stay, you will avoid some of the miscommunication that can occur. Also, if you are dealing with a complaint, asking why the guest believes they are not getting what they thought they would can also allow you to reset any incorrect expectations that they may have.

Recognise Feelings

When something doesn't go to plan for a guest, make sure you acknowledge how they feel. This is an important element in building trust that can sometimes be overlooked. You might not overlook this intentionally; you could be busy or just focused on dealing with the situation the guest has flagged with you. But when you take the time to recognise their feelings about the situation, and thank them for bringing it to your attention, you can turn the situation into a positive for you and the guest. Our business has received many 5-star reviews because we acknowledged a guest's feelings, therefore making the guest feel good about bringing the problem to our attention.

Be More than a Pretty Picture

One way you can get a guest offside before they even walk into your reception is if your business looks nothing like the photographs on your website or social media. Your online presence must look as close to what your business appears in person as possible. You have an obligation to ensure that what a potential guest sees online is what they will get in reality.

Guests will accept slight variations, like if there are a few marks on the wall because you painted your rooms three years ago or you have slightly scuffed carpets. Even the biggest hotel chains suffer from wear and tear, and guests understand this. However, if you show beautifully manicured gardens and facilities in your photographs online, but you actually have overgrown grass, weedy garden beds, overflowing bins and dirty facilities, their trust will immediately disappear.

Remember that the trust relationship you have with a guest begins before they even book with you; it starts when they are researching your business. So make sure that your business delivers on what you promise; match your online presence with your real-life presence. No-one likes a fake online profile.

There are many other small ways that you can build trust with a client, but these are some methods that have worked incredibly well for me. The more you focus on building trust with your guests through open, individual, honest, curious, clear, empathetic and personal interactions, the more successful you will set your business up to be. And if your guests trust you, then they will demonstrate this trust to others by becoming Promoters of your business, rather than Detractors.

A Resource for You

Finding ways to deliver a personalised approach for your guests can be a difficult task. You're close to your business, so you might feel that what you already provide is just what your guests need and want.

However, there are a few simple ways that you can add a personal touch to your business, ranging from cheap to relatively expensive. Of course, any updates you invest in will need to be weighed against the return that change will give you; however, there is almost no accounting for the benefits that providing incredible customer service can have for your business.

Below you'll find some great ways to create a personalised service in specific areas of your business.

At Check-in

- Provide reception staff with a full list of the day's expected arrivals.
- Ensure that staff use guest names when addressing them.
- Tailor welcome packs for individual guests: ask for your guest's favourite foods and recreational activities during sign-in and recommend local restaurants or sightseeing experiences near your business.
- Welcome repeat guests back in a special way: check the notes from previous bookings and use that information to make them feel valued.
- Have staff forward book guests into local restaurants.
- Have umbrellas on hand for guests to use during rainy weather.
- Offer a free caravan parking service.
- Provide access to free wi-fi.
- Offer free branded stubby/drink holders or other merchandise.

During Their Stay

- Welcome guests with personalised, handwritten greeting cards in their rooms.

- Offer a turndown service.
- Provide chocolates and cleaning cards in rooms after cleaning.
- Offer green cleaning processes on request.
- Provide a list of entertainment options, like board games, that you have available at reception.
- Provide a list of daily activities in and around your business.
- Provide daily weather and/or surf reports.
- Offer vouchers for local businesses.
- Have items available at reception that guests might need during their stay, such as sunscreen or ice (you can charge a small fee).
- Take time to walk around your park and engage with guests.
- Provide free garbage and recycling bags.

At Check-out

- Say goodbye with an inexpensive gift, for example, a small chocolate, to thank guests for their stay.
- Ask where they are headed and offer directions to a local tourist spot.
- Give a departure pack, either in person or electronically.
- Offer to help move bags to their car.

CHAPTER 12

Grab the Bull by the Horns

The 2 guys we saw and spoke to during our stay were very pleasant easy going friendly and helpful Can't ask for more Sorry, I don't remember their names Coming back next year with some other families if they can get spots Thank you

~ Allison

The best way to avoid bad reviews appearing online about your business is to just not get any.

Let that sink in a little.

I can hear your thoughts running through your mind from here:

I've already had bad reviews – how can I not get any?

I just had a guest who is guaranteed to leave a bad review – it's too late now.

You're crazy! You can't please everyone!

Or can you?

When I tell my clients this I'm usually met with looks of confusion. The reality is there is a way, several in fact, that you can avoid receiving bad reviews while your guests are still at your business.

My R.E.V.I.E.W. process has allowed my clients to take the bull by the proverbial horns, meet their guests head-on and stop the bad review cycle from impacting on their businesses.

You don't need to have the best facilities in the world or the most amazing location on earth either.

Sure, those things will help, but there are plenty of businesses that have average facilities in okay locations.

What I'm talking about is a way to put reviews in front of your guests before they leave, and I am talking about the service you provide to every guest that enters your door. There are ways that you can facilitate guests not only raving about their experience when they leave, but also during their stay and make sure that other guests have the best experience too.

I am talking about the holy grail – the Promoter. In the last two chapters I showed you methods in my process that can help you deal with your guests in the digital world of social media and review sites, and how establishing trust is the foundation to growing your business. Throughout this chapter I will take you through several options in building your business around guests who will work alongside you, cementing the momentum of change.

Find Your Promoters

The first thing we need to get straight is that you won't be able to turn every guest into an advocate for your business. That's just the way it is. Some of your guests will just want to arrive, enjoy what you have on offer and then leave. There is no point spending time going after every single guest that comes into your business. The following steps will give you the know-how you need to find your Promoters.

Step One: Guest Engagement

The first place to find your Promoters is through engagement with your guests. Logical, really! What you are looking for are guests who ask questions, guests who are genuinely interested in how your business runs and where they can find everything they need. These guests have the potential to be Promoters because they are actively engaged with your business when they arrive and during their stay. They will ask your team about their day and they will engage in a conversation with you.

Step Two: Social Media

The second place to find your Promoters is through social media. Pay special attention to names that appear regularly across your social media platforms, especially ones who 'like', 'comment' and 'share' your posts. These guests are again already engaged with your business and at the tipping point of becoming brand advocates.

Your review sites are also a great place to find people who are rating your business 4–5-stars. Your 3-star reviewers are also possible advocates, however take the time to read their commentary as they could just be your middle-of-the-road guest who won't move up into an advocate status.

Step Three: Returning Guests

The third place to look for Promoters is through your repeat guests. If you cross-reference these guests with the first and second steps to find guests who have given you 3-star reviews, they may have the potential to be an advocate for your business. Any guest who returns to your business regularly obviously likes something about it to make them happy to stay again. This could be your proximity to landmarks and beaches, your price point, or the ease at which they can travel to your location. There are a lot of reasons why you have repeat guests. Knowing these reasons can help to drive them into being brand advocates for your business.

The Gold-Star List

You will now have a gold-star list of guests who are already Promoters or who have the potential to be with a little work. It is normal for this list to be small; depending on the size of your business, it could be anywhere from 10 to 50 people. The number of advocates you have does not need to be big, because it's the reach of the advocate on social media that is significant. Brand advocates are four times more likely to participate on feedback sites and discussion boards and 75 per cent more likely to share their positive experiences online.[6] So you can see it is well worth your time and investment to find and nurture your Promoters.

You should also try to profile certain attributes about guests on your gold-star list. This will help you work on attracting more advocates who fit that same profile.

Roll Out the Red Carpet

Once you have identified the typical profile of your Promoter guests and your list of past 3-star reviewer guests for Promoter targeting, it's time to work through the following proven strategies to push Passives into Promoters, and Promoters into VIP guests.

Create a Unique Experience

Sure, you could spend a wad of cash on your guests to create unique experiences for them, but this might not actually turn them into a Promoter for your business. You can create a unique experience just by showing the guest that they are important to your business and not just any other guest. Little things like a handwritten welcome card left in their room works well at creating a personal experience for return guests.

Offer a Phenomenal Customer Experience

The single, most proven technique to turn any guest into a Promoter is through a winning customer experience. When you deliver on promises, treat guests with respect and kindness, welcome them with a smile and engage them in conversation, you exceed expectations and create an engaging experience that wins hearts. The more you look for ways to help a guest during their stay, the better the experience is for them. Having a kick-arse customer experience will also give you leeway when it comes to tired facilities or if things go wrong.

Create a Loyalty Program

One of the best ways to create repeat business, while at the same time creating Promoters, is through a loyalty program. This program doesn't need to result in a free night's accommodation (or it could). Instead, you could offer other types of rewards, like free breakfast or a VIP welcome pack after a certain number of stays. Whatever it is that your bottom line can accommodate, I would highly encourage you to build a loyalty program for your business.

Supercharge Your Loyalty Program

Once you have a loyalty program in place, find a way to supercharge it. What do I mean by supercharge? Let's take, for example, a loyalty program for a coffee shop. The loyalty card has eight spaces for a stamp to be added whenever a coffee is bought and the ninth coffee is free. I'm sure we are all familiar with this standard loyalty program.

Supercharging this type of program would be as simple as providing a card with ten spaces for stamps with the eleventh coffee free, but you handing the card over to the customer with two stamps already on it. At the end of the day, the number of coffees the customer needs to purchase before receiving a free one is still eight, but they believe they are getting better value because they originally received two free stamps. Studies on this approach to loyalty programs have found that those with the free stamps have a 34 per cent higher chance of guests returning to the business. So supercharge away![7]

Be Honest and Active

There will be times in your business when problems occur. There is no getting around that. This does not have to be the end of your mission to turn a guest into a Promoter, though. The more honest and upfront you are about the error that has occurred, the better chance you have of turning them into an advocate for your brand. There is an important caveat to being honest with guests though; you must action what they are advising you to do. If you are honest with them about a problem and don't act on it – you will easily turn them into a Detractor.

Ask for Feedback

I believe that asking for feedback and reviews is the number one way to create Promoters for your business. This is because your guests benefit from your hard work and dedication to your business's output. There really is no-one better placed than your guests to tell you where things need to improve. And asking guests proactively for feedback allows you to get on top of any potential bad reviews long before they hit online. I have created a few different ways to collect feedback from guests throughout their stay and after they leave. These include the Mid-stay Survey, social media training, conversations with guests and the After-departure Survey.

Are You Working or Are You Chatting?

My wife, Casey, has an inbuilt radar and when I'm out chatting to guests I often warn them that it is very likely that she will call and ask: 'Are you working or are you chatting?'.

Now I put a strong emphasis on getting feedback straight from the horse's mouth, so to say. I make an effort to get around my businesses, and whenever an opportunity presents itself, I chat to guests and hear amazing snippets of information. One example was a couple that had an extraordinary caravan with a fold-down deck over the drawbar. My opening gambit was to compliment them on the van and how much of a practical use of space it was. We chatted a bit more and they returned a compliment about how much they liked the layout of our amenity block.

Now, when someone gives me a nice comment, I am not scared to turn that into a positive review. I asked them if they would mind putting a review on their favourite review site or, at the very least, including their kind words in our After-departure Survey. By the time I got back to the office, they had left two great reviews online and were clearly Promoters, and I got to demonstrate to Casey that 'chatting is working'.

The Mid-stay Survey

While my guests are in the middle of their stay, I send them a survey about how their experience has been so far. This tells me if there is anything that might need improving while they are still at the business, so that I can address it before it becomes a bigger issue.

These surveys do not have the same return rate as After-departure Surveys, however those that are returned give me valuable insights into my guests. It also gives the team the opportunity to address any concerns before they become issues, and help give the guest the recognition they deserve.

Social Media Training

My business offers free half-hour social media training sessions for guests three times a week. These were implemented mainly from the amount of questions staff were receiving from guests about how to use their phones, tablets and Facebook accounts. The training sessions show guests how their devices and social media accounts work. This usually works best for our grey nomad guests, so it won't work for all demographics. We ask attendees if they wouldn't mind leaving us a review, and it always results in positive feedback for the business.

Conversations with Guests

Whenever my team or I engage in conversation with a guest in the park, we always take the time to ask how their stay is going. This simple question can lead to guests giving positive and negative feedback, and can sometimes give good insights into how we can improve things across the business. It also demonstrates to our guests that we value their input, and can help us turn a Passive guest into a Promoter. Never underestimate the power of a quick conversation.

The After-departure Survey

Once a guest has left our business we email a survey requesting feedback about their stay. This survey is a great way to avoid feedback being left in public forums. It can also allow guests to open a dialogue with you that they may have felt uncomfortable with while still staying with you. Some businesses will tell you that you should wait a few days after guests depart to send out your survey; however, my return rate is much better, and more positive, when sent on the same day as departure.

A Resource for You

In this chapter, I've discussed ways to avoid bad reviews appearing about your business by finding, encouraging and retaining Promoters.

We also talked about using surveys and conversations with guests to locate your Promoters and deliver them the VIP treatment.

All this information can leverage off the questions you include in your departure surveys; however knowing the best questions to ask can sometimes stump business owners.

Before I jump into these questions, I'll give you a few caveats so that you have a good participation rate in your feedback surveys.

Survey Caveats

Caveat 1: Try not to have too many questions; don't have any more than six or guests simply won't fill the survey out. Also there is nothing more frustrating for your guests to be forced to answer questions, so resist the temptation to make your questions mandatory.

Caveat 2: Wherever you can, give guests questions that are easily answered with a rating or a yes or no. If you ask them to write a response, you will likely see low participation rates and vague answers. The more you help your guests by providing specific options, the more responses you will receive.

Caveat 3: Always give your guests the option to be contacted about their survey results, then follow up within two days of receiving their responses.

Caveat 4: Send your After-departure Survey on the day your guests depart, or within the first 24 hours, as you will have a better return rate than if you wait for a few days.

Sample Questions for Your Survey

On a scale of 1 to 10 (10 being the best):

Q1. How likely is it that you would recommend <insert name> Holiday Park to a friend or colleague?

Q2. Feel free to provide comments on why you provided this response.

Q3. What do you like most about <insert name> Holiday Park?

Q4. What do you like least about <insert name> Holiday Park?

Q5. What is your age?

Q6. How would you describe yourself and/or the purpose of you last visit?

Q7. Do you want to be contacted by one of our friendly staff about your responses to this survey?

Q8. Please provide your preferred contact method i.e. email, phone number.

CHAPTER 13

Create Leaders, Not Followers

Great Staff!!!!!! Your office staff are the face of your company, and yours were extremely helpful, fun, and informative. Clean, well run park. Great location.

~ David

If you look at most companies on a review site you'll often see the following pattern emerge:

Your staff were incredibly rude.

It was a great trip except for the horrible way staff treated our family.

Never returning, the staff were awful.

Location was great, but Beryl on reception needs to retire, rude woman.

Poor Beryl.

You can have the best facilities in the world, have a great product and offer competitive prices, but the one thing that guests will not forgive is being treated in a rude or disrespectful way by you or your team.

Sometimes, this feedback can be taken with a grain of salt and let go, but either way, the guest will always need a response that requires a little finesse. This is where we enter the land of grey. Sometimes guests are in the wrong, or are looking for a refund. If they are declined that refund request this can be taken as rude even if you and your team are incredibly respectful in the way you handled the matter.

There can also be times when your staff are rude unintentionally – they are at work, after all, and can have moments where they are just too busy to give guests the time they feel they deserve. There are times when being a human being gets the better of us and we are rude – that happens, but not as much as guests advise.

The one thing that I make sure of is that I have a great team working around me so that I minimise the amount of feedback that my businesses receive on this issue. The added benefit of having a great group of people around me also means that my businesses deliver an outstanding level of customer service that far outweighs the occasional bit of negative guest feedback.

An important element of my process is looking at my clients' teams and finding ways that they can carry on the methods that I help implement. I remind my clients that the successful outcome of the changes introduced into their operations are largely undertaken by their team. Upskilling or setting up a great team isn't all that difficult; it just takes patience, time and a passion to deliver to your team a great experience, just as much as you want to deliver one to your guests.

Empowering for Success

I've had many different jobs in my life, but the jobs I look back at fondly all had one element in common – empowerment – and this is something I strive to give my team members. I know this sounds like a bit of a kumbaya word, and brings up images of hugs and high-fives and team building. But, at the heart of it, empowering your staff means you give them freedom to make decisions about completing their day-to-day tasks, while also making them responsible for those decisions and their outcomes. No-one, anywhere, enjoys having someone hover over them, dictating how to do something. And if you have the time to do that, then who is running your business?

I can relate to being concerned or worried about how a member of your team may go about their job. But at the end of the day, their performance comes down to you and how well you've trained them for their role. I've found that there are a few additional processes that you can put in place to ensure that you give your team the freedom they need, while minimising the risk of situations going awry. It's all through empowering your team.

But it's also important to set boundaries. For example, requesting that your team members are careful with equipment. Especially if they are driving a golf buggy around your business and they leave the keys in the ignition, and then decide to walk away from it for a while. They may just find that some kids will take it for a joyride. Yeah, it pays to make sure that your team keep an eye on things.

Make Your Expectations Clear

Giving people the freedom to make decisions does not mean letting them take control of any situation without a framework to work in. Communicating your expectations on how staff should operate is the first step in creating a successfully empowered team. I find the best way to do this is via situation-based discussion: I provide a scenario to the team and ask how they would deal with it. This way, I can gauge their responses and correct any approaches I don't think will work or are not in alignment with how I would address them.

I don't second-guess my team in front of one another; instead, I offer alternative suggestions and encourage them to comment on my suggestions. That way, we feel like we are all involved, rather than having me dictate responses to them. I also make a point of refreshing these expectations after a new situation has occurred in the business, so that the team can see some live examples.

Set Up One-on-ones

Taking the time to sit with your individual team members and have a discussion with them about their role is a great way to ensure that you are across the way they make decisions. You can choose to have these chats formally, with meeting minutes and action items for each of you if you prefer. Or you can go grab a coffee and have an informal chat. There is no rule on how a one-on-one needs to be completed.

One thing I will flag is to try to make sure the chat is not all about business. Talk about your team member's personal life, their likes and interests as well. The more you get to know your team personally, the more their dedication to you and to their role will be reinforced.

Have Your Team's Back

There will be situations that won't be appropriate for your team to deal with. In my businesses, this is when guests are being rude to my team. I have a zero-tolerance policy for abusive behaviour, and I make sure that team members know there is no reason they should be involved in situations where they feel threatened. This policy shows my team that I have their back, and will step in and help them out when needed.

I also make a point of never dressing down, or putting a team member in a situation where they feel undermined in front of a guest or another member of the team. If there has been an error made, I will deal with the situation and then talk to the individual in private to ensure that they don't feel embarrassed. No-one is going to make the best calls all the time, myself included, so I find that giving my team the respect that I would want is the best way to deal with situations that haven't worked out too well.

Building the Best Team

It is one thing to set up your team to ensure they perform at their best – it is a totally different ball game to set up a team who are passionate about their jobs and want to come to work every day.

Building a loyal and dedicated team takes extra work, but the payoff is a business that provides the best customer service that you can only dream about. Over the years, I have created a team of people who are just as passionate and dedicated to the success of the businesses as I am. There are a few key items that have contributed to this, and they are not all that difficult to implement.

Be as Flexible as You Can

Anyone who has kids and works can tell you that unforeseen things happen; as a parent you are occasionally having to decide between work and kids. When these situations occur, I make sure that we are flexible enough to move rosters around, allow team members to leave work early, or bring kids into the office.

I even offer changes to rosters for some team members around things that they enjoy doing in their downtime. I have a team member who loves fishing, and occasionally I'll ask him if he wants a roster change on a weekend of good weather so he can go fishing in the morning. It makes no negative impact to the business, but it does mean I have a team member who is grateful and refreshed.

This flexibility means that I have a team that knows I care about them beyond them coming in to work every day, and, in turn, they are less stressed and able to perform well in their jobs.

Always Celebrate the Wins

My businesses and teams receive the occasional bad review, but most of our feedback is positive – and a lot of our guests make a point of singling out individual team members for their good work. We make sure we acknowledge these wins by having a weekly call out where we read out the feedback left by guests and collectively celebrate as a team. I know my team works hard, so showing them their impact on the business goes a long way in building a brilliant team.

My business has also been nominated for and won some great business awards. When these fantastic moments happen, I bring along the team to the awards night, at my cost, to allow them to celebrate the win with me. This is also a great way to build a good rapport with the team outside of work.

Invest in Your Team's Success

Taking the time to understand how your team members want to develop professionally and then looking for ways that you can help them achieve this is one of the best return on investments for your business. That's not to say you should allow your team to attend training courses that you pay for without a commitment back to you. We have a policy that if we pay for training then team members must remain in the business for at least 12 months after the training is completed, otherwise we expect them to contribute to the cost of the training if they leave early.

Of course, investing in your staff doesn't need to cost you anything. If you are prepared to give up a little bit of your own time, sit down with team members and train them on new tasks or functions. This can result in a mutual benefit: you can delegate tasks while the staff member progresses in their professional development. The more you demonstrate your willingness to give them greater responsibilities, the more dedicated your team will be to you and your business. Don't have time to train staff yourself? Then there is a way to use technology to streamline the process which is covered in the next chapter.

It's All About the Trust

I've found that there's one other effective way to build a dedicated team: showing your team how much you trust them by asking their opinions on business operations. What do they think of the new colour scheme you are thinking of implementing in the rooms? What do they think about building a new playground or installing a pool? What kind of booking system should you use in the business?

Another fantastic way to show your team trust is by being honest. Don't be afraid to make mistakes in front of them, and be up-front when you've made a mistake. No-one is perfect. If you never acknowledge that you are infallible, then you run the risk of ostracising yourself from your team.

At the heart of every great relationship is trust. The more you trust your team, the more they will trust you.

A Mini Task for You

In this chapter, I talked about building your team members' confidence in making decisions and setting the playing field for how you want your business, and team, to operate. I walked you through how to set expectations and implement these across your business to ensure that your team operate, not only as you want them to, but in a way that brings out the best in them.

Having a great team is not something that happens overnight - it takes time and patience. A great way to set yourself up for success is by creating a set of 'Core Company Values', and involving your team in creating them by following seven easy steps.

Step 1

You will need to create a master list of 50-100 company values that will form the starting point for this task. I found plenty of examples by searching online for the terms 'core company values' or 'list of core values'.

Step 2

Depending on the size of your business, arrange for your management team – a handful of your high-achieving team members or even your whole team if it's small – and arrange a time to have a workshop with them. Ideally you will want 4-8 people to participate. This exercise is best completed in person, but can also be completed remotely via Skype or email if your team is not local. Don't let distance prevent you from completing the task.

Step 3

Distribute your master list and ask each team member to refine the list to 8-12 values that they think are most important to your business. I find the easiest way to help in this process is to think of someone in your business or industry who is really good at what they do. Now think of what qualities this person has that makes them so successful. If you have trouble thinking of someone related to your business or industry, then use someone who inspires you, or you look up to, as your reference.

Step 4

On a whiteboard or big pieces of paper so that everyone in the group can see them, list down the values that each person has chosen and discuss their reasons for including these values. To really push this home, have members of the team capture the ideas from the group.

Step 5

Now that you have the information documented, have the group look for common themes or values. Generally I find that there are at least a few values that keep recurring.

You will be left with a list of values that you can incorporate into your own business operations. Ideally, you will have a total of 4–6 values that resonate with your team. Bonus points if you can get your core values to form an acronym! This will assist in helping you and your team to remember and readily recall the core values.

Step 6

Buy a nice picture frame (don't skimp on it!). Create a single page that lists your Core Company Values and print it out in colour. Frame your values and put them up where your customers and team can see them and refer to them.

Step 7

Emphasise the importance of your Core Company Values across your business. I make it clear to all my staff that if they make a decision with the core values in mind and can explain their reasoning to me, they will never be disciplined for that decision. Talk about staff empowerment. My staff don't hesitate to show initiative as they have clear guidelines to help their decision-making process.

Our core values are in our recruitment process, in our newsletters, attached to staff rosters, in the reception area and in the staff break room. The staff hold each other accountable and, instead of petty squabbling, they self-regulate. If a staff member is not respecting the values, then other staff can call them on it. And you know what? It isn't personal – it is clear what is expected.

By taking your team through this exercise you will find a common set of rules that will underpin what is deemed to be acceptable or not, and it will be something the team will incorporate into their day-to-day work as they will feel a sense of ownership over how each value is implemented in the business.

A Note on This Approach

In the workshop situation, there may be some members of your team who are hesitant to commit to providing answers. Take note of these staff members and discuss this with them away from the group. Hesitation could be due to them not wanting to participate in the process, or it could be a comfort issue. Not everyone is comfortable in committing to approaches that will be ingrained into the business operations, so it is worth your time to explore their reluctance further in an unthreatening environment. But do note that for this process to work, it requires the whole team to engage with the outcome.

Empowering staff

I had a manager working in my team who I had complete confidence in, but who felt they had to check every decision they made with me. This resulted in me having to spend too much of my own time managing their responsibilities.

Through consultation I discovered that they were fearful of making a mistake, and this lead to potential impacts on the business and their position. We implemented the Core Company Values and almost immediately they felt empowered and free to make decisions without retribution.

The manager empowered his own team that lead to a new era of autonomy which freed up his time, and helped him become a more thorough and competent manager.

CHAPTER 14

Embrace the Tech

Codes for ammenities tended to be a little confusing

~ Malcolm

I remember the days before smartphones and the internet. It was a wonderful time where people really connected with each other, and we held hands and skipped in fields of long grass.

Running a business was simple. It wasn't complicated at all and your guests loved you all the time.

Right?

Of course that's a load of crap.

If anything, technology has made the world a place that is more connected than ever before. Today you can talk face to face with someone living in Antarctica! You can talk to someone in SPACE!

Technology has also given people who run their own businesses the capability to do more and achieve more. It has even made it possible for small businesses to go toe-to-toe with large corporations and beat them in the same industry. Today's technology makes everything an even playing field for people running a business.

Technology can also really help you tackle negative reviews and ensure that your business is able to create a solid group of loyal and engaged guests that will come to your defence online and in the real world.

Technology can also provide you with ways to automate tasks in your operations, allowing you and your team to focus on the human element of your business, and build connections and relationships with your guests.

If you're not embracing technology, then, quite frankly, you're going to be left behind and your business will fall into obscurity.

Today is the day you should stand up and embrace the next phase of your business and lead the charge. You truly are only limited by your imagination when it comes to technology.

A lot of my clients become concerned when I start to walk them through the technology options that are available to them in this area of the R.E.V.I.E.W. process. I'm always brutally honest with them and admit that even I struggle at times with technology; I prefer things to be simple. Over the years of developing my process, I've found that the best approaches are the ones that save you time and allow you to focus on the really important things, like making sure that my guests are getting the best experience and my team is running as effectively as possible. The reality is, without technology it just isn't possible to stay on top of everything AND build your business AND stay in front of your competition.

The best part of all is, you don't have to break the bank to do it.

Putting Your Best Digital Face Forward: Your Website

There is no point getting into the technical aspects of leading in the business world today unless we take a little time to talk about websites. If you're in the accommodation business and you don't have one, you seriously have rocks in your head.

A website is so much more than just a digital business card; it is your own little part of the internet where you can control everything. You can control comments left for you, you can control bookings, you can control every aspect of how you want the world to see your business and what it offers. And, with a little bit of work, you can even make sure that most of your guests visit your website before they go to the other websites that come up in a Google search.

There are, of course, a few fundamentals that a website needs to have to really push you forward: being user-friendly and linked to your booking system.

Make Sure Your Website is User-friendly

We have all visited websites that overwhelm us with information, flashing graphics and dense writing – and every one of us has clicked right back off those websites. The best kind of websites are easy on the eyes, get right to the point and are easy to navigate.

There are three key things that people want to know when they come to a website:

1. who you are
2. how to contact you
3. how to book with you.

Everything else on your site is window dressing.

Don't get me wrong. Making sure your website is pretty and shows off your business is important, but aesthetics take a back seat to these three key things. When you build a website, make sure that you have that very simple list at the front of your mind to ensure that users get what they come for.

Make Sure Your Website is Linked to Your Booking System

If a guest visits your website they are there for two main reasons: to check out your products, and to make a booking with you. If you don't have an option to book directly through your website, then you open yourself up to a loss of income. For example, if your guests are directed through your website to book through a site like TripAdvisor, then you lose out on the full rate you would have received because of the commission you must pay to the booking agent.

Making sure they can book with you directly is smart business sense. It also allows your guests to book 24/7 rather than having to wait for office hours to call and book over the phone.

Think Outside the Box

Having a well-planned website is a good step towards embracing technology, but you can also use your website as a way for guests to interact with you while staying at your business. You can make it a central information location for guests to find directions around your area, or discounts at local restaurants or tourist sites. You can also use it as the noticeboard for activities or events that you have on. You can even set it up as a place for your own guests to leave electronic notes for each other. There is no limit to what you can do with your own website. The more relevant it is for your guests, the better it will serve your business.

Help Your Guests Embrace Tech

One of the best things you can do for your guests is to make sure that they are changed for the better in some way after they leave your business. Sounds like a tall order, right? But the fact is, most people think fondly of their family vacations. These are the times they can just relax and let the rest of the world go. The times where they spend time with friends and family, and share happy experiences, rather than finishing work for the day, paying a bill or buying a car for the family. Holidays are all about human connection.

To further promote these connections, we adopted a strategy to help our guests connect with us and their loved ones using technology. Every week we offer three half-hour classes where we teach guests the basics of social media. Managing accommodation parks on the coast of NSW means that we have a big demographic of guests who fall into the grey-nomad category. Even though these guests do have the latest smartphones or tablets, most of them are not proficient at using social media.

Sharing our knowledge with our guests has given them the ability to interact with their families while they are on the road. Plus it has created a fantastic word-of-mouth situation for our bookings. We incorporate a section in the classes which asks participants to jump onto the business's social media pages to review listings and leave a review for us. When this is done right in the middle of us helping them, it leads to great reviews that have driven our own ratings up on these sites.

This is one of the simplest ways we have found to provide a quality service for our guests that is not offered by our competitors, and means that we have a solid market differentiator. It goes far beyond just providing guests with access to free wi-fi. It gives guests a skill to take away that they wouldn't have expected to receive when they book with us.

Use Tech to Automate Your Guest Engagements

Running a business is filled with a lot of tasks that take up time. I'm talking here, of course, about paperwork and administration.

Your focus and your team's is constantly taken away from your guests to get these tasks done. But there are ways that technology can help minimise time impacts to your business or, in some cases, completely take over the running of these tasks.

When your guests book with you, it is standard practice to send a confirmation of their booking. This is typically a receipt and details of what they've booked. But this can be so much more than just a confirmation. You can use this process to automate paper-work, like providing additional information that your guests need to know when they arrive, through to pool opening and closing times. You can even use this process to send regular updates on what is happening in the area, leading into their stay with you.

This is where having the right booking system can really work to your advantage. There are several on the market and the system you choose will come down to preference. However, I recommend making sure that the system you go with has the capability to easily export your database, as this is an essential tool for marketing your business.

Email Marketing and Your Database

An email nurture campaign allows you, as a business, to develop specifically targeted email marketing that is driven by how your guests respond to an initial email. When I first heard about email nurture campaigns I nearly fell off my seat. Finding out that there is a way to automate your communications with guests based on their behaviour opened my eyes to even more ways of taking busi-ness to the next level.

For example, say you want to send an email to guests who stayed with you two years ago but haven't returned to your business since. You can send an initial email offering a value-add proposition, such as not charging for an additional child on their next booking. The system that generated the email is then able to track the number of guests who opened the email, how many clicked on details in that email and what was clicked on. It can even track those who may have made a tentative booking but did not complete it.

What your email marketing system is then able to do is generate follow-up emails with specific messages encouraging guests to move through to a final booking. In the example of those who almost made a booking, the system can start sending emails with a count-down advising that the discount will only last another three days. This will usually encourage a few of the past guests to complete their booking.

Of course, this system does need to be approached with a bit of common sense. You don't want to spam your past guests as that might turn them off staying with you. However, if you are clever with your communications and offer value to these guests, the return on investment that you can achieve with email marketing is astronomical.

Use Email Automation to Create Promoters

We talked in a previous chapter about creating brand ambassadors and making your guests Promoters of your business. One of the simplest ways to do this is by using your email marketing system to generate guest emails based on special occasions, such as guests birthdays. Most booking systems have the ability to store the birth-date information needed to generate these emails, so combine this with a well-written email and your email platform can help you to create a unique, feel-good piece of customer service to win your guests' loyalty.

Improve Your Customer Service with Tech

Another handy thing that technology provides is multiple communication avenues for guests to interact with your business. The more lines of communication you have, the better placed you are to take advantage of booking opportunities. I would highly encourage any accommodation business to consider adding live-chat capabilities to their website. These allow you to communicate directly with people who are visiting your website. This approach is starting to gain traction with many service-based industries as a highly effective conversation tool.

We also make a point of engaging with guests who follow our Facebook page with our reception team responding as quickly as possible to messages that are posted.

A Resource for You

In this chapter, I touched on some modern-world technologies that I use to improve and automate my business.

However, there is so much more technology available to utilise, and it really comes down to personal preference, and your business's strengths and weaknesses to determine what is beneficial to you to integrate into your business. As such, I've put together a brief list of some available options that you can investigate in your own time. While the following list does cover some options I use myself, please be aware that technology changes at a rapid pace and other alternatives may now be available at the time you're reading this book.

Please note, I'm not endorsing the following products, but rather giving you an invitation to do some research on what would be best for your particular circumstance. For more options, check out the resources section.

Project Management/Organisational Options

Trello (www.trello.com): Trello has a variety of work and personal uses including real estate management, software project management, school bulletin boards, lesson planning, and law office case management. I use Trello in my own businesses to readily record and distribute information.

Asana (www.asana.com): I believe this is one of the best project management tools available; it is one of the most used and has the same functions as Trello – plus unlimited storage.

Communication Options

Slack (www.slack.com): This platform includes features such as group and private messaging, images and videos, rich link summaries, and notifications. I use Slack to communicate with my teams at different sites.

Azendoo (www.azendoo.com): Azendoo is a team collaboration platform. Chat centers around one topic that can include documents and images. Communication happens in the comments, so each group of conversations is already filtered for relevance.

Email Campaign Options

MailChimp (www.mailchimp.com): This is an email marketing service that allows people to send email newsletters, invitations, reminders and more to lists of subscribers.

GetResponse (www.getresponse.com): GetResponse is an email marketing platform. It enables you to create a valuable marketing list of prospects, partners and clients, so you can develop relationships with them and build a responsive and profitable customer base.

Outsourcing Options

Fiverr (www.fiverr.com): A global online marketplace offering tasks and services, beginning at a cost of $5 per job performed, from which it gets its name. The site is primarily used by freelancers who use Fiverr to offer services to customers worldwide.

Upwork (www.upwork.com): On Upwork, you'll find a range of top talent, from programmers to designers, writers, customer support reps, and more. It's the world's largest online workplace where savvy businesses and professional freelancers go to work.

Survey Options

SurveyMonkey (www.surveymonkey.com): This platform is used to launch a variety of online survey projects for different purposes, such as getting employee or customer feedback, competitive analysis, quick polls and market research. I use SurveyMonkey in my businesses for guest and staff surveys.

SurveyGizmo (www.surveygizmo.com): A platform that makes it simple for users to create and conduct all types of questionnaires, quizzes, polls and surveys.

Booking System Options

NewBook (www.newbook.cloud): Founded in 2010, NewBook was designed as a property management solution for the accommodation industry. It specifically uses the cloud and has a strong focus on innovation. It is very intuitive and easy to use. Its reporting features are excellent for those who like to keep up to date on how their business is performing. I use NewBook in my business.

RMS (www.rmscloud.com): RMS has a long history of providing a quality and robust reservation system to the industry. It is a great system with an excellent reputation. I use RMS in my businesses.

Extra Options

Camtasia (www.techsmith.com/video-editor): This is a screen recorder and editor that captures all your on-screen activity and turns it into an engaging video for you to share with the world. I use Camtasia to record training videos, issue instructional videos and record meetings.

Voice Recorder: Almost all smartphones have the ability to record snippets of audio for when you need it at a later date. Voice Recorder is a great tool for quickly recording important things or situations. I couldn't live without the voice recorder on my phone.

Skype (www.skype.com): This is a VoIP service, which uses the internet to allow people to make and receive free voice and video calls online for free or at a low cost. I use Skype often to communicate with a range of people.

Vivino (www.vivino.com): This is an online wine community, database and mobile application where users can buy, rate and review wines. It is great for finding good wines for Promotor guests. At the end of the day, a good wine can make all the difference.

LastPass (www.lastpass.com): This is a freemium password management service that stores encrypted passwords in private accounts. LastPass is standard with a web interface, but also includes plug-ins for many web browsers and apps for many smartphones. It also includes support for bookmarklets. LastPass has changed my life: one password to rule them all.

Zapier (www.zapier.com): This is an online automation tool that connects your favourite apps, such as Gmail, Slack, MailChimp and over 1,000 more. You can connect two or more apps to automate repetitive tasks without coding or relying on developers to build the integration. I use 'Zaps' in my businesses.

CHAPTER 15

Can I Get a Process?

Thank you for being so helpful in the booking process.
It was helpful that we could add extra people onto the site
on the day and pay then.

~ Jillian

Making sure your business is set up to operate at its best capacity is fundamental for business success.

However, this isn't something that just happens.

It takes a lot of hard work, and for those business owners who are at the top of their game, the hard work never ends.

Being successful at business means that you are constantly evolving and making sure that today is better than yesterday, and that what you learn every day guides you through the decisions you need to make for tomorrow.

The key ingredients that ensure your business is taking the right steps forward are the processes you have in place. Processes will lay out exactly what steps are needed to achieve the best outcome. You should have processes that cover your team, from hiring to firing, to everything in-between. You should have processes that cover your guests, from checking-in to checking-out in the best way, to capturing personal details and payment information, to generating surveys.

There should be processes for buying cleaning products, for creating rosters, for cleaning facilities and the grounds of your business. There are dozens of processes that ensure your business runs effectively and efficiently and these should appear to your guests as magic that happens around them.

Processes also allow you to pinpoint where a breakdown has happened in the running of your business, and allows you to put measures in place to avoid the same incident from occurring again.

But the truth is, processes will break down, things will be missed and things will go wrong. It is highly likely that this will impact on someone who has come to experience your business. How you respond to these situations demonstrates the passion you have for your business and your guests. And when you take this passion and put in place process changes, you ensure that your business will be a leader in your industry.

This brings me to the two crucial elements of the R.E.V.I.E.W. process: the I: Implement Changes Based on Feedback E: Evaluate the Impact of the Change steps, which rely on my clients developing and introducing key processes into their organisation structures. This is where the methods I roll out find their feet and help my clients to take their businesses into a new mode of operation. I tell my clients that if it isn't written down, then it doesn't exist. It is too easy for team members to say they 'weren't aware' they had a responsibility to perform a certain task, opening their business up to poor guest experiences. At its core, my process enables my clients to build methods that allow their businesses to work efficiently and effectively, in turn creating incredible experiences for their guests and positive impact on revenue.

What Processes Work the Best?

Every business is different, and every business owner runs things differently, but that doesn't mean there aren't universal processes that work well across all businesses and will set you up for success. When I step in to manage a new business, the first thing I look for are documented processes. To this day, I am still surprised at how many businesses, from small to large operations, don't have basic processes documented. It's great if your office assistant knows how they go about their day-to-day work, but what happens if they leave? You lose all the knowledge essential for the business's operation. The following are some processes that will assist in the smooth operation of your business.

Make Sure Everything is Documented

Documenting the essential tools that you need to run your business sounds basic, and you're right, it is. However, there are many businesses that don't have the essentials mapped out in easily accessible processes. I recommend using a cloud-based collaboration tool like Trello to store your systems and processes. Making a point of also having a super-user access to all the computers in your business is also a wise move. The last thing you want is for an essential member of your team to leave the business, and you are now unable to log on to the computer and manage your bookings.

Even if you are a small operation, these days we all have so many usernames and passwords for multiple systems that it becomes almost impossible to keep track of them all. Use a password manager like LastPass as the repository for all your login details. This is a modern method of writing passwords down and keeping them in a secure place, like the office safe. I have used LastPass for approximately three years and it has changed my life; it is safe, secure and easy to use.

Onboarding and Training Processes

Anyone who has had the experience of training new team members will tell you that it can be an incredibly rewarding and incredibly painful thing to go through. When you have hired a new team member, you are likely to be in a situation where someone has left or you are busy enough to need an extra pair of hands. Often you don't have time to go through every single task with the new staff member. This is where having documented job processes comes in handy. It ensures that essential information is not overlooked and makes clear to the new team member what is required. They will get up to speed to assist you in your business in a much quicker time frame.

By having your business's processes and essential policies documented, the onboarding experience is a lot easier to manage. You can also block out times when you know the existing team isn't as busy to give the new member some practical hands-on exposure to their tasks. In my business, I use key milestone sign-off points for new team members to show their understanding of processes. This avoids problems down the line if they state they weren't told how a task needed to be completed. A way to save time in delivering onboarding and training processes is to use software like Camtasia to create a recording of the key electronic processes that you repeat often. Even if you prefer to deliver the training in person, by giving your staff access to a recording of the session means they are able to revisit the training when needed to ensure it sinks in and makes sense.

Standard Quality Processes

Making sure that your business runs smoothly and that each guest's experience is of the highest quality requires a uniform approach to the way your business is presented. For example, your guests will expect your rooms to be clean when they arrive, and the camping grounds to have closely mowed grass so that they can pitch their tents in a nice location. Specific processes make sure your team delivers on these expectations.

One of the biggest gripes that guests will have is about the cleanliness of your business. If you have a specific room-cleaning process in place, you ensure that items won't be missed and you are more likely to avoid receiving complaints. This means your cleaners can follow a strict process such as: change the bedsheets, vacuum the floor, clean the bathroom, empty the bins, and finish with replacing the towels. However, if you do receive complaints, having a specific process means you will easily be able to spot where the process failed, and remind your team how things need to be done.

Using Processes to Ensure Success

As we have discussed many times in this book so far, bad reviews are a gift to you as a business owner. They highlight where things have gone wrong and what needs to be addressed. They can also highlight areas where you might not have a process which you can then develop. There are a few fundamental things you can do to ensure you make the most out of the feedback that your guests give you.

Gather Feedback From Your Guests

This is probably obvious by now, but the one thing I want to ensure is engraved on your brain after reading this book is that you must gather feedback from your guests. You can do this from surveying your guests during or after their stay with you. You can get feedback from multiple online sources: review sites, social media and your own website. If you don't already gather feedback from these places, then start – today! If you want to start by using only one source of feedback, then go ahead. Just make sure you start somewhere.

Listen to the Feedback

It's one thing to read the feedback you have been given; it is another to listen to it. Try, as much as you can, to move beyond the negative feelings you get from feedback. Read earlier chapters and run through some of the exercises to cope with the emotional cycle that comes from feedback.

It is hard running a business and there are a lot of other people in the same industry as you. If you want to step ahead of your competition, one of the simplest and most inexpensive ways to do this is simply by listening. You must listen to what your guests are saying and make sure you are incorporating their feedback into your current processes. This is one of the easiest ways that your business can grow and improve.

Walk in Your Guests' Shoes

You don't have to wait for guests to give you feedback to make improvements to your processes. Regularly taking a walk in your guests' shoes can help your business to improve year on year and build a solid group of loyal and repeat guests. All you need to do is experience your business as they do and ask yourself, 'Is this the kind of service that is top rate?' The truth is, you are probably going to be a lot more critical of your own business than your guests will ever be, so if you are delivering a service that YOU rate highly, then you will deliver something that is truly spectacular to your guests.

Don't Ignore Inefficiencies

It's one thing to have processes that ensure tasks get completed correctly; it is another to have processes that hamper your business's success. There will be times when something unfortunate happens in your business and you will need to change the way things are done to avoid that situation from happening again. But if that situation was a one-off, and the new process now means double the work, then it probably isn't an efficient change to your processes.

Likewise, you might have a process in place that worked when you had half the guests you do today, but now that your business is highly successful the process is now either redundant or it doesn't meet the standards you expect. If that's the case, ditch it. There is nothing worse than holding on to an outdated process that ultimately doesn't meet your expectations, or those of your guests.

Have a Review and Audit Procedure

Having documented and well thought out processes is the foundation of an effective and lucrative business that is loved by your team and your guests. Making sure that there is also an audit process that allows you to evaluate the effectiveness and completion of operational processes is also essential. Don't assume that everything you outline for your team is being completed the way you expect.

I audit our processes about every six months by asking my team how things are going and listening to what they say. As they are the ones managing the processes, they are in the best position to advise me on their effectiveness. Every two to three months, I also randomly check my teams' work output to ensure that processes are being followed in the way they are laid out. These are simple ways that I can ensure my business processes are the best they can be.

A Mini Task for You

In the last chapter I covered ways that you can set up your business for success by having robust processes in place. A mistake that business owners can make is approaching every task in their business with a sense of unconscious confidence.

This is something that works against documenting and creating processes that can help your team deliver the way you want them to, and can also mean you take longer to implement processes because the information is stored entirely in your head.

With this chapter's mini task, I will help you find where your unconscious confidence comes from. Once you are aware of this, you will be in a position to provide your team with documented processes that will set your team and business up for success.

You can choose to do this task in one of three ways: you can use paper and pen, you can record your responses, or you can video yourself and watch/listen back when you need. If you do record your responses (voice or video), then I would recommend engaging one of the tech options from the previous chapter, like Fiverr or Upwork, to get it transcribed.

Ready? Let's get started.

Step 1: Think about a task that you do that no-one does better than you – it can be anything at all.

Step 2: Ask yourself, 'What do I do that's better than anyone else?' and 'What makes my approach unique?'

Step 3: Take a moment to reflect on why you believe you do it better than anyone else. What do other people do that makes the outcomes less successful? Make sure you write these reasons down.

Step 4: Thinking about your approach, how could you teach someone to do that task as well as, or better, than you do it? Record the steps to do this.

Once you have all of your responses documented you will be most of the way to creating a document that you can use to underpin all of your processes.

Capturing the magic that you deliver into your business is the best way you can ensure success across your business at all times. It will be the backbone of your growth and will ensure that you drive your business forward year after year.

PART FOUR

THE
LAST PART

CHAPTER 16

A Final Piece of Advice

Always enjoy our stay, well priced, excellent Managers
and Staff, very convenient, what more could we ask for?
- Murray

When I first started looking at reviews for the first business I managed, I'll admit that I struggled. I couldn't understand why guests who were coming to stay with us couldn't see the hard work and time that went into giving them the best experience I could. But the reality is they never will see that effort.

Guests will not see that the reason their bin didn't get emptied is because the team member cleaning their room was distracted by a fight they had with their partner that morning. The guest will only see that their bin wasn't emptied.

Guests won't know that the reason their booking went missing was because you just upgraded your booking system and were led down the garden path by the IT company who did the upgrade. All they will know is that you lost their booking and their holiday got off to a rocky start.

Guests won't care that their meal arrived on the lukewarm side of cold because their waitress cut her finger after she took their order and was delayed getting the meal to the table. They only care that now they must wait while it goes back to the kitchen to be heated up.

What I am getting at here is that every guest that enters your business has only one thing that they see, know and care about: themselves. They expect that you will provide them with the experience that they deserve, not the one you think they want to have. This is by and large where every bad review you will get comes from: you didn't meet your guest's expectations, even if you were never in a position to meet those expectations in the first place.

Understanding this is how I found my freedom from bad reviews and started to embrace them.

You see, the guests giving you bad reviews don't consider any of the blood, sweat and tears that went into creating the place they want to visit and return to. Their bad review isn't personal. The reviewer doesn't consider you as a person, or your team as individuals. The reviewer's only consideration is themselves.

Now don't get me wrong. I'm not saying you should throw out your marketing plan and ignore your demographic research and just deliver your business whichever way you want. Those things are still incredibly important, and are essential in you knowing and understanding how to deliver the kind of services and experiences you want to deliver. But you do need to let go of all the other baggage that comes with a bad review. Mistakes will happen, and things will go wrong. That's life. Get over it and get on with it.

If you're still concerned about what the reviews are telling you, ask yourself, why? Why are you procrastinating about dealing with them? Why are you defensive about what they say? Could you have handled that situation better? Is that team member not delivering, and should you let them go? Is the feedback you are getting from your guests right?

Great. Now you have a starting point to improve your business. You can make it a better version of itself and you don't need to spend thousands of dollars to have someone tell you the areas that need improvement. Your guests are already giving you this advice for free.

The truth is, no business is perfect and no business will deliver everything to everyone every day – and that isn't something you shouldn't try; if you try to please everyone, then you'll end up pleasing no-one.

The last, age-old simple piece of advice that I'd like to share with you is what I always come back to when I struggle with feedback, or I'm looking at making a change to my business or starting a new business. It's a simple question.

What if it was me?

If you find yourself locked in a struggle with your inner voice about who was right or wrong in a situation that a guest gave feedback on, ask yourself, 'What if it was me?' If you're struggling to find the right response to some feedback online, ask yourself, 'What if it was me?'

The more you put yourself in your guests' shoes and see things from their perspective, the better you will be at dealing with the situation and the feedback they give you. When you look at your business from the eyes of your guests, you will start to see it in a new light. You will notice new ways to provide better service. You will find it easier to use social media platforms that target your guests. You will be a better leader for your team and take them to new heights in their careers because you will continually reinforce the core values that drive your business and make them better at what they do.

Making changes to your business and embracing technology will become less daunting and expensive because you will understand that it will give your guests a better experience and enhance their stay. The better you understand your guests, the easier it will be to engage with them, proactively ask them for feedback and create Promoters who will help you to create a successful and engaging experience for as many guests as possible.

The sooner you realise that you will always get bad reviews and look at them for the wonderful, positive gifts that they are, the sooner you can take your business to the next level and win guests time and again.

Keep in mind that no matter how bad the review is, your guests' worst day on holiday should still be better than their worst day they have had in the real world.

Acknowledgements

I'd like to take a small moment of your time to acknowledge some important people who have been involved in my book writing journey. This list is not supposed to be exhaustive and I am sure there are those out there who deserve some credit whom I don't mention, and to you I am grateful for your assistance.

First and foremost is my family, Casey, Harley, Blake and Zoe. You are the reason for everything. Thanks for providing the inspiration and drive to help me handle the difficult days, but also for helping grumpy daddy become happy daddy when he needed to.

Amplify Agency, you guys rock. Shout out to my brother in crime Ronsley. Keep doing what you are doing mate and inspiring those around you. I never thought I could ever be comfortable with someone else in my head, but Shannon you do it so well. Thanks for all your help and poking and prodding in a way that ensured I got what was in my head onto paper. Wouldn't have happened without you guys.

My family and close friends. You have all helped in your own special way, even if you haven't realised it. I appreciate the relationships I have with each one of you.

BG5 and others that I have maintained contact with during my KPI journey. You guys know who you are.

Ann Wilson from Independent Ink, one of my BG5 buddies. Thanks for making the book real. I'll never forget when I got it back from you after being typeset and thinking, Holy s*&t this thing is real.

All those staff, guests and clients who have ever given me good or bad reviews. I have used all your feedback to help me grow myself and my businesses. I have harnessed the power of your feedback to achieve some amazing results, of which I am very proud and very thankful.

To work with Adrian and implement his
6-step REVIEW framework in your business go to
www.thatbadreview.com or email
hello@adrianeasdown.com
Feel free to leave Adrian a review about this book on the website.

That Bad Review Podcast

For weekly insights, great advice, implementable processes and
real-life stories of working in the accommodation and hospitality
industry, subscribe to Adrian's weekly podcast.

That Bad Review

Available on iTunes, stitcher, Spotify and all other
great locations of audio.

B1G1 – Business for Good and the Power of Giving

We all have the ability to make a difference and I believe in the
power of habitual giving. I pledge that for every sale of my book
I will make an impact through giving via B1G1.

The project that will benefit from every sale of the *That Bad
Review* book is to provide a learning hub to indigenous youth.
The project can be found at
https://www.b1g1.com/projectdetail/455 and is described as:

*Help a young person living in a remote indigenous community to
develop IT and English literacy skills by providing a safe space for one
day, for enhanced learning and capacity building. The provision of a
hub for community engagement helps its members to overcome barriers
of learning and develops the ability of individuals to participate in the
social and working life of the community.*

You can find more information about B1G1 at www.b1g1.com or
listen to my podcast on That Bad Review with Paul Dunn, the
chairman of B1G1 at www.adrianeasdown.com/paul-dunn

Resources

For those interested in even more tech options, here is an extended list to check out.

Project Management/Organisational Options

Airtable

This system is similar to Microsoft Excel spreadsheets, except you don't need to learn all of the functions and shortcuts.

Avaza

This system combines project management capability with accounting software and is a great one for connecting project teams with their suppliers and external clients.

ClickUp

ClickUp is in the same vein as Trello; however, useful artificial intelligence is included, making it a standout for project management tools. You will need to pay for this one, though.

Kanban Tool

This system is used by companies such as Xerox, Cisco and Expedia for its in-built security features that keeps your information secure, while providing great virtual interaction for project management. This one's for those serious about working virtually on big projects.

Yalla

Another great project management tool, Yalla combines ease of use, accessibility and built-in time-tracking and communication tools. This one is popular with laid-back start-ups and the younger gen.

Communication Options

Bitrix24

This platform goes above and beyond with no limit on search history, completely free video conferencing, and free screen sharing. Bitrix24 also has built-in tasks, document management and CRM features.

EXo Platform

Beyond traditional chat functions, EXo offers an all-in-one reference system, where a company can host wikis, task management, project management, forums and even document management.

Fleep

A platform that enables you to send messages to anyone with an email address – no more 'walled gardens' where you can only chat with other people on your platform. If you're sick of asking people to sign up for different chat platforms just so they can communicate, Fleep is a great option.

Jostle

This is a platform that clarifies workplace teams, makes internal communication happen at all levels, and surfaces information/expertise across the organisation. For virtual businesses, it becomes the go-to place to participate in workplace culture, understand organisational goals, and celebrate success.

Email Campaign Options
SparkPost

SnarkPost is the world's number one email infrastructure provider and the most performant email delivery service available. It is the cloud-based transactional email solution from Message Systems and is designed specifically for developers.

ActiveCampaign

This is an intelligent platform that makes it easy to leverage marketing automation. You'll be able to design sophisticated, auto-mated marketing processes that save time and generate additional revenue for your company. I use ActiveCampaign in my businesses to provide information and to nurture my guests.

Maropost

An on-demand email marketing provider specialising in increasing one-to-one customer engagement and optimising email marketing performance.

AWeber

An email solution for small business marketers who don't have a lot of time to spend on their email marketing campaigns.

Emma

You can create truly beautiful emails with Emma's 200+ templates that stand out among all the email marketing services. And when they custom design a template for you, it looks very professional.

Outsourcing Options

Airtasker

This Sydney-based company provides an online and mobile market-place enabling users to outsource everyday tasks. Users describe the task and indicate a budget, and community members then bid to complete the task.

Survey Options

QuestionPro

A web-based survey solution that lets you easily create online surveys and polls and share them with your target audience.

Getfeedback

This system is ideal for a range of feedback scenarios including pre-event surveys, post-event surveys, employee feedback, customer feedback and business partner surveys.

KeySurvey

A platform that collects feedback from customers, market research, employee engagement, and enterprise feedback management.

QuickTapSurvey

This solution is great if you wish to create surveys and gather responses offline using Android and iPad tablets. Data capture can occur anywhere and does not need access to the internet to record responses.

Notes

1   https://www.brightlocal.com/learn/local-consumer-review-survey/
     http://www.tripadvisor.in/pdfs/OnlineTravelReviewReport.pdf
2   https://www.businessinsider.com.au/tripadvisor-affects-tourism-of-entire-countries-2015-3
3   https://www.linkedin.com/pulse/20130604134550-284615-15-statistics-that-should-
     change-the-business-world-but-haven-t/
     https://www.helpscout.net/75-customer-service-facts-quotes-statistics/
     http://leeresources.com/
     https://beyondphilosophy.com/15-statistics-that-should-change-the-business-world-but-
     havent/
4   https://searchengineland.com/eye-tracking-study-everybody-looks-at-organic-listings-
     but-most-ignore-paid-ads-on-right-67698
     https://www.searchenginejournal.com/24-eye-popping-seo-statistics/42665/
5   https://blog.bufferapp.com/3rd-party-social-media-tools
6   http://adage.com/article/cmo-strategy/marketers-court-brand-advocates/228279/
     https://www.infusionsoft.com/business-success-blog/customer-service/
     customer-experience/turn-your-customers-into-an-army-of-brand-advocates
7   https://www.helpscout.net/blog/customer-loyalty-programs/